TREES AND BUSHES

IN WOOD AND HEDGEROW

by Helge Vedel and Johan Lange

translated by C. H. R. HILLMAN, M.A., DIP. FOR.
adapted by H. L. EDLIN, B.SC., DIP. FOR.

EYRE METHUEN LTD
11 NEW FETTER LANE, LONDON EC4P 4EE

First published by Politikens Forlag, Copenhagen
in 1958 as *Træer og Buske I Skov og Hegn*
© 1958 by Politikens Forlag
English translation © 1960 by Methuen & Co Ltd
Reprinted four times
Reprinted 1973

Plates printed in Denmark

Text reprinted by photolithography in Great Britain
by Cox and Wyman Ltd, Fakenham, Norfolk

S.B.N. 413 30160 5

INTRODUCTION

The aim of *Trees and Bushes in Wood and Hedgerow* is to describe the appearance and character of all the wild trees and shrubs found in Britain's open countryside; the majority of the numerous introduced trees grown only in parks, gardens, and botanical collections, are purposely omitted. This is a practical handbook for the country-lover and forester alike, an indispensable guide to all our native woodland and hedgerow species.

The close similarity between our own flora and that of Scandinavia has made it possible for this outstanding Danish book to be adapted to suit British conditions. Botanists visiting northern Europe will also find that it contains most of the species of tree and shrub that they are likely to find in the field.

The book is conveniently divided for easy reference. From the illustrated keys a tree or bush may be simply identified by its leaves or related character. A note on the keys explains their use for beginners.

The 96 pages of lifelike coloured plates set new standards for both botanical illustration and colour reproduction. Depicting 120 different trees and shrubs in some 440 separate sketches they show the form of the whole tree, the smaller details that interest the botanist and aid identification, the tree's place in the landscape, and some of the uses of the timber. The trees are arranged according to their botanical classification, so that nearly related kinds appear close together. The English name given is that which is most commonly used or is most explicit; the current Latin scientific name appears in italics. In the captions to the illustrations the sizes of the subjects are indicated: $\times 1$ means that the drawing is full size; reductions and magnifications are similarly shown, e.g. $\times \frac{1}{2}$, $\times 4$, etc.

Each of the species described has a reference number. This is used throughout the book in the coloured plates, the descriptive text, and the index.

The main text consists of descriptions of trees and bushes. A section is devoted to each of 127 species. It contains notes on nomenclature, botanical description, biology, habitat, utilization, and distribution. Line illustrations are used to explain botanical details, and maps show places of origin.

The book also includes accounts of wood structure, tree nutrition, forestry development, tree breeding, and many other useful and fascinating items.

The originators of this book have said that their wish is to spread scientific knowledge of trees and shrubs among all who encounter them, and they express the hope that it may give the same pleasure to its readers as they themselves derived from compiling the text and painting the remarkable pictures.

The illustrations and the layout of the text are the work of Ebbe Sunesen and Preben Dahlstrøm. With the exception of numbers 3b and 49c, which are based on *Bäume und Sträucher des Waldes* by Hempel and Wilhelm, all the plates were drawn from living specimens.

The description of each tree is preceded by an account of the origin and development of its name, or names. These accounts were prepared for the original Danish version by Johan Lange, and have been adapted by H. L. Edlin.

The text was written by Helge Vedel. C. H. R. Hillman made the English translation; H. L. Edlin adapted and edited the work as a whole to make it more suitable for the woodlands and hedgerows of the British Isles.

Thanks are due to Johan Lange for advice and assistance with the compilation of the text; to Dr C. Syrach Larsen for supplying specimens from the Charlottenlund Forest Garden and the Hørsholm Arboretum; to Professor K. Gram for the maps showing the distribution of each kind of tree; to Professor V. M. Mikkelsen for the pollen frequency diagram, and to M. V. Knudsen for information on the uses of the various sorts of wood. A. F. Mitchell, of the Forestry Commission Research Branch, has kindly provided most of the records of Britain's tallest and stoutest trees.

Works referred to in the preparation of the English edition include:

Clapham, A. R., Tutin, T. G., Warburg, E. F., *Flora of the British Isles*, 1952.
Dallimore, W., Jackson, A. B., *A Handbook of Coniferae*, 1931.
Druce, G. C., *Hayward's Botanist's Pocket Book*, 1926.
Edlin, H. L., *British Woodland Trees*, 1945; *The Living Forest*, 1958.
Elwes, H. J., Henry, A., *The Trees of Great Britain and Ireland*, 1913.
Fitschen, Jost, *Gehölzflora*, 1955.
Gilbert-Carter, H., *British Trees and Shrubs*, 1936.
Hadfield, Miles, *British Trees*, 1957.
Harlow, W. M., Harrar, E. S., *Textbook of Dendrology*, 1941.
Loudon, J. C., *Trees and Shrubs*, 1875.
Rehder, A., *Manual of Cultivated Trees and Shrubs*, 1947.

H. L. EDLIN

CONTENTS

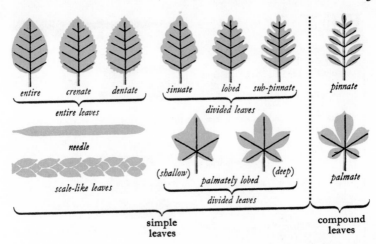

entire   *crenate*   *dentate*   *sinuate*   *lobed*   *sub-pinnate*   *pinnate*

entire leaves   *divided leaves*

needle

scale-like leaves   *(shallow)* *palmately lobed* *(deep)*   *palmate*

divided leaves

simple
leaves

compound
leaves

KEYS *for the identification of trees and bushes by their leaves.*

These keys are arranged so that, starting from the Main Key, you proceed step by step until the plant is identified. According to the leaf's characteristics, you make a choice between the alternatives in the first bracket. The figure in heavy type refers you to another bracket, and so on until the species is named. A page reference to the appropriate coloured illustration is given after the name of the species. Where some explanation of a botanical term may be needed in the keys, an illustration is given, and the glossary may also be consulted (p. 220).

As with all such keys, this one cannot be entirely comprehensive, but it will enable the reader to identify nearly all of the species illustrated in this book.

MAIN KEY

1 { Leaves needle- or scale-like ....see **KEY I** page 6

Leaves with blades .... see **2**

2 { Leaves opposite .... see **3**

Leaves alternate .... see **4**

3 { Leaves opposite, compound ....see **KEY II** page 8

Leaves opposite, simple ....see **KEY III** page 8

4 { Leaves alternate, compound ....see **KEY IV** page 10

Leaves alternate, simple ....see **KEY V** page 11

KEY I

Branches with needle-like or scale-like leaves

1
- Leaves needle-like .... see **2**
- Leaves scale-like .... see **19**

2
- Needles long (1–6 in.), in closely set bundles with 2 or 5 in each bundle................. ...(Pines) see **3**
- Needles shorter (½–1½ in.), some in clusters on dwarf shoots, and others singly on long shoots .(Larches) see **9**
- Needles in whorls of 3, awl-shaped .... **Juniper** (pages 34–35)
- Needles single .... see **10**

3
- 2 needles in each bundle .... see **4**
- 5 needles in each bundle .... see **8**

4
- Cones and side branches only at the tip of each year's long shoot .... see **6**
- Cones and side branches also in the middle of the more vigorous long shoots .... see **5**

5
- Needles about 1 in. long, twisted. Cones pointed, twisted, light greyish-brown, without prickles on scales .... **Jack pine** (page 30)
- Needles 1–4 in. long, very wide, slightly twisted. Cones more or less oblique, brown, with small prickles on scales ....**Lodgepole pine** (page 30)

6
- Needles bluish-green, 1–3 in. long. Bark on stem and older branches reddish-yellow. Cones dull greyish-green, stalked .... **Scots pine** (page 28)
- Needles dark green, bark not reddish. Cones without stalks .... see **7**

7
- Needles short (1–3 in.), not prickly; cone scales brown and shiny ....**Mountain pine** (page 29)
- Needles long (3–6 in.), prickly ....**Austrian pine** (page 29)

8
- Young shoots slightly hairy; cones 3–8 in. long, slender, banana-shaped ....**Weymouth pine** (page 32)
- Young shoots thickly brown-felted, cones 2–3 in. long, barrel-shaped ....**Cembran pine** (page 31)

9
Cone scales with edges rolled back; needles bluish-green. Long shoots reddish violet to slightly glaucous ....**Japanese larch** (page 27)

Cone scales straight (not rolled back); needles light green. Long shoots pale yellow to yellowish-brown .... **European larch** (pages 26–27)

10
Needles with prominent midrib on the dark green upper-side, under-side pale green. No cones, but pea-sized seeds with red seed-coat ....**Yew** (page 17)

Needles without prominent midrib on upper-side, flat or 4-angled. Trees with cones .... see **11**

11
Needles with wide, rounded leaf base. Leaf scars rounded, level with surface of branch. Buds plump, cones erect ....(Silver firs) see **12**

Needle-bearing areas more or less prominent. Leaf scars not level with surface of branch .... see **15**

12
Needles green on upper-side, 2 whitish stripes on under-side .... see **13**

Needles dull bluish-green to green on both sides, on under-side of branches closely spaced, twisted and curved outwards and upwards ....**Noble fir** (page 20)

13
Needles evenly parted to two sides, shoots therefore flat .... see **14**

Needles not evenly parted, some directed forwards, shoots arched on upper-side ....**Caucasian fir** (page 19)

14
Needles long, up to 2 in. Young branches almost glabrous, with yellowish-brown bark ....**Giant fir** (page 21)

Needles short, up to 1 in. Young branches with short dark hairs, and greenish bark....................**Silver fir** (page 18)

15
Needle-bearing areas only slightly prominent. Buds pointed. Needles with evenly tapered stalks. ...**Douglas fir** (pages 24–25)

Needle-bearing areas clearly prominent. Needles with distinct stalks .... see **16**

16
Needles with short green stalks which fall with the needles .... **Western hemlock** (page 25)

Needles with brownish stalks which remain on the branches ....(Spruce) see **17**

17
Needles very prickly, flat, whitish-blue on under-side. Cones with soft, projecting, wavy-edged scales.................... ...**Sitka spruce** (page 24)

Needles not nearly so prickly, 4-sided to compressed. Cones with firm, adpressed, rounded scales .... see **18**

18	Needles pure green, shiny. Cones 2½–6 in. long	**Norway spruce** (pages 22–23)
	Needles dull greyish-green to bluish-grey. Cones about 2 in. long	**White spruce** (page 23)

19	Cones, globular, about ¼ in. wide, with shield-like scales. Under-side of shoots green or with pale whitish-grey spots	**Lawson cypress** (page 34)
	Cones about ½ in. long, with overlapping scales. Shoots on the under-side either lighter green or with well defined greyish-green areas	(American cedars) see **20**

20	Leaves with prominent glands, under-surfaces of shoots light green	....**White cedar** (page 33)
	Leaf glands indistinct, under-surfaces of shoots with greyish-green areas	**Western red cedar** (page 33)

KEY II

Branches with opposite compound leaves

1	Leaves palmate, with 5–7 leaflets	..**Horse chestnut** (page 95)
	Leaves pinnate	see **2**

2	Terminal bud black, 7–11 leaflets, pith small	**Ash** (pages 104–105)
	Terminal bud greyish-brown, 5–7 leaflets, pith large	see **3**

3	Pith white, flowers in flat umbel-like inflorescences, fruit black	..**Common elder** (pages 108–109)
	Pith yellowish-brown, flowers in egg-shaped to rounded inflorescences, fruits red	**Red-berried elder** (pages 108–109)

KEY III

Branches with opposite simple leaves

1	Leaves palmately lobed	see **2**
	Leaves entire (simple)	see **5**

2 { Leaf stalk up to 1 in. long with glands; white flowers in flat umbellate inflorescences; red fruits .... **Guelder rose** (page 109)

Leaf stalk longer, without glands. Winged fruits. (Maple family) see **3**

3 { Leaf under-sides bluish-green, eventually reddish. Buds and green parts without milky juice .... **Sycamore** (page 93)

Both leaf surfaces fresh green, milky juice in buds and green parts .... see **4**

4 { Under-surfaces of leaves glabrous, leaves with 5–7 lobes, acuminate, with 3–5 teeth, incisions rounded .... **Norway maple** (page 92)

Under-surfaces of leaves downy, leaves smaller, 3–5 blunt lobes, incisions pointed .... **Field maple** (page 94)

5 { Leaves heart-shaped, entire, glabrous. Fruit a brown capsule .... **Lilac** (pages 106–107)

Leaves lance-shaped, entire, brightly glabrous. White flowers. Black berries .... **Privet** (pages 106–107)

Leaves narrowly tongue-shaped, leathery. The plant has forked branches and grows on stems and branches of other trees .... **Mistletoe** (pages 161-162)

Leaves elliptical, oval or egg-shaped .... see **6**

6 { Leaves with finely serrated edges .... see **7**

Leaves entire-edged .... see **8**

7 { Leaves elliptical-oval, with 3 pairs of curved lateral veins. Branches often with spines .... **Purging buckthorn** (page 96)

Leaves elliptical, with 7–10 pairs of straight lateral veins. Branches without spines .... **Spindle tree** (page 91)

8 { Leaves with 3–5 pairs of curved lateral veins, acuminate. Flowers in umbel-like inflorescences ..... **Dogwood** (page 103)

Leaf veins not curved, flowers either in pairs or in small bunches .... see **9**

9 { Plants twining or creeping along the ground with long yellowish to reddish flowers in bunches .... **Honeysuckle** (pages 110–111)

Bushes without twining or creeping shoots .... see **10**

10 { Leaves and young shoots glabrous. Reddish-white flowers, white berries .... **Snowberry** (page 110)

Leaves and young shoots downy. Yellowish-white flowers .... see **11**

11 { Stem bark ash-grey. Red berries .... **Woody honeysuckle** (page 112)

Stem bark reddish-brown; dark blue glaucous berries .... **Blue-berried honeysuckle** (page 111)

KEY IV

Branches with alternate compound leaves

1	Leaves palmate	see **2**
	Leaves pinnate	see **4**
2	Leaves with 3 leaflets (sometimes single as in broom and gorse)	see **3**
	Leaves with 3–7 leaflets, with arched shoots (runners) with strong prickles	**Blackberry** (page 76)
3	Leaflets ovate, 1–3 in. long, shoots and fruits glaucous; fruits with scattered weak prickles resemble blackberries. Low plants with arched runners	**Dewberry** (page 77)
	Upright plants with slightly prickly bristles, leaves with snow-white under-sides. Red fruits	**Raspberry** (page 75)
	Leaflets lance-shaped, up to ½ in. long. Branches twig-like, green, edged	**Broom** (pages 88–89)
	Leaflets only normally developed in young plants and on very vigorous shoots, otherwise developed into very sharp thorns	**Gorse** (page 89)
4	Leaflets entire-edged. Young vigorous branches with spines (stipule spines) in pairs	**Robinia** (page 87)
	Leaflets serrated	see **5**
5	Branches with weak bristles, leaves with 3–7 leaflets having snow-white under-surfaces. Red fruits	**Raspberry** (page 75)
	Branches with prickles	**Roses** see **7**
	Branches without prickles	see **6**
6	Leaflets oblong-lanceolate, 2–4 in. long, 13–24 leaflets..........................	**Sorbaria** (page 67)
	Leaflets oval, 1–2 in. long, 9–15 leaflets........	**Rowan** (page 70)
7	With sickle-shaped prickles	see **8**
	With straight prickles and bristles............	see **9**
8	Leaf with glands on under-surfaces and margins, leaves smelling of apples or grapes	**Sweet briar** (page 79)
	Leaves glabrous, without glands, unscented	**Dog rose** (page 78)
9	Leaflets ½–1 in. long, glabrous. Small black hips	**Burnet rose** (page 78)
	Leaflets 1–2 in. long, downy. Large flattened red hips	**Ramanas rose** (page 79)

7

KEY V

Branches with alternate simple leaves

1	Leaves lobed	see **2**
	Leaves simple (entire)	see **15**
2	Leaves palmately veined and lobed	see **3**
	Leaves pinnately veined, sinuately lobed or sub-pinnate	see **8**
3	Evergreen plants, creeping or climbing with adventitious roots	**Ivy** (page 102)
	Bushes or trees without creeping or climbing shoots	see **4**
4	Leaf under-surfaces with snow-white felt, trees	**White poplar** (page 39)
	Leaf under-surfaces without snow-white felt, bushes	see **5**
5	Branches with thorns.....................	**Gooseberry** (page 66)
	Branches without thorns	see **6**
6	Under-surfaces of leaves with small yellow glands, aromatic scent. Black berries	**Black currant** (page 65)
	Under-surfaces of leaves without glands. Red berries	see **7**
7	Leaves small, 3-lobed, under-surfaces shining, inflorescences upright	...**Alpine currant** (page 66)
	Leaves larger, 3–5 lobed, hanging inflorescences	**Red currant** (page 65)
8	Under-surfaces of leaves with dense hairs, or felted	see **9**
	Under-surfaces of leaves glabrous or only slightly hairy	see **11**
9	Under-surfaces of leaves chalk-white felted	**White poplar** (page 39)
	Under-surfaces of leaves grey felted	**Whitebeams** see **10**
10	Leaves pinnately lobed................	**Swedish whitebeam** (page 72)
	Leaves with pinnatisect base and sub-pinnate to pinnately lobed apex	**Finnish whitebeam** (pages 72–73)
11	Leaves up to 2 in. long, bushes or trees usually with spines	...(**Hawthorns**) see **12**
	Leaves over 2 in. long	see **13**

12
Lowest lateral veins of leaf curving forwards, leaf usually lobed .... **Midland hawthorn** (pages 68–69)

Lowest lateral veins of leaf curving backwards, leaf pinnately lobed to pinnatafid.............. **Common hawthorn** (page 69)

13
Leaves with pointed lobes wedge-shaped base, buds brown .... **Red oak** (page 61)

Leaves with rounded lobes, buds brown .... see **14**

Leaves 5–7 lobed with deep, pointed lobes, buds green .... **Wild service tree** (pages 72–73)

14
Leaves short-stalked, buds short, plump. Acorns with long stalks............................. **Pedunculate oak** (pages 58–59)

Leaves long-stalked, buds slender, pointed. Acorns almost stalkless .... **Sessile oak** (page 60)

15
Buds with only one hood-like bud scale ....(Willows) see **16**

Buds with several scales, or without actual scales........................... see **23**

16
Branches glaucous in places .... **Caspian willow** (pages 46–47)

Branches not glaucous .... see **17**

17
Leaves glabrous or only slightly hairy .... see **18**

Leaves hairy, especially on under-surfaces .... see **19**

18
Upper-surfaces of leaves light green with stomata (visible with lens), under-surfaces of leaves greyish, twigs with very brittle base........................**Crack willow** (pages 46–47)

Upper-surfaces of leaves without stomata (lens), upper and under leaf-surfaces darker green, shiny, branches not particularly brittle at base ....**Bay-leaved willow** (page 48)

19
Leaves 1½–4 in. wide, often ovate, with grey-felted under-surfaces......................... ...**Goat willow** (page 44)

Leaves narrower .... see **20**

20
Leaves linear-lanceolate, 4–10 in. long, with rolled-in margins and silver glistening under-surfaces .... **Common osier** (pages 46–47)

Leaves lance-shaped, 1½–4 in. long, with compressed silky hairs on both sides. Stomata on upper surfaces (visible with lens) .... **White willow** (pages 46–47)

Leaves 1–4 in. long, without stomata on upper-surfaces (lens) .... see **21**

	Dense hairs on buds and shoots	see **22**
21	Buds and previous year's shoots reddish; glabrous or almost smooth. Grey hairs on under-surfaces of leaves, tips of leaves often twisted...............	**Eared willow** (page 45)
22	Leaf under-surfaces grey-felted, leaves slightly serrated, tips of leaves often twisted	...**Grey willow** (page 45)
	Under-surfaces of leaves glistening with silky hairs, leaves entire-edged. Low creeping shrub	**Creeping willow** (pages 46–47)
23	Length of leaf more than 3 times the width ..	see **24**
	Length of leaf less than 3 times the width	see **30**
24	Branches and leaf under-surfaces silver glistening. Leaves linear. Thorny and thickly branched bush	**Sea buckthorn** (page 101)
	Branches and leaf under-surfaces not silver glistening	see **25**
25	Leaves narrow, with rust-red felt on under-surfaces............................	**Wild rosemary** (page 102)
	Leaves without rust-red felt on under-surfaces	see **26**
26	Leaves entire-edged	see **27**
	Leaves with more or less serrated edges	see **28**
27	Leaves greyish-green, tall bush with long, slender, pendulous, light-grey branches armed with spines	.....**Tea tree** (page 107)
	Leaves with bluish-green under-surfaces and green upper-surfaces, low bush with stiff branches	.....**Daphne** (page 100)
28	Thick bush with many spines, white flowers, dark blue fruits	**Blackthorn** (page 80)
	Bush without spines	see **29**
29	Leaf-edge serrated only near apex, scented when rubbed	...**Sweet gale** (page 49)
	Whole leaf-edge finely serrated, without scent ..	**Willow-leaved spiraea** (page 67)
30	Leaves grey- or white-felted on under-surfaces (in grey poplar this usually applies only to leaves of suckers and furthest leaves of long shoots)	see **31**
	Leaves not felted on under-surfaces	see **35**
31	Leaves entire	(Cotoneasters) see **32**
	Leaves sinuate-dentate or crenate	see **33**
32	Upper-surfaces of leaves glabrous, fruits red	**Cotoneaster** (page 67)
	Upper-surfaces of leaves hairy, fruits black.........	**Cotoneaster melanocarpa** (page 159)

33 {

Leaf-edges doubly serrated, with dense white felt on under-surfaces .... **Whitebeam** (pages 70–71)

Leaf-edges doubly serrated, with loose grey felt on under-surfaces ....**Grey alder** (page 53)

Leaf-edges sinuate-dentate .... see **34**

34 {

Under-surfaces of leaves felted snow-white, leaves on vigorous shoots 5-lobed ....**White poplar** (page 39)

Leaf under-surfaces with less dense grey felt (often missing on older leaves), leaves on vigorous shoots not 5-lobed .... **Grey poplar** (pages 40–41)

35 {

Leaves thick, leathery, shiny dark green, usually with thorn-toothed margins ....**Holly** (page 90)

Leaves otherwise .... see **36**

36 {

Leaves entire-edged .... see **37**

Leaves with crenate edges .... see **39**

37 {

Leaves regularly pinnately veined, with veins extending to leaf margins .... see **38**

Leaves irregularly pinnately veined, with veins forked near leaf margins. Leaves leathery, shiny dark green, plant usually climbing on trees or walls ....**Ivy** (page 102)

38 {

Buds slender, pointed, with many scales ....**Beech** (pages 56–57)

Buds without actual scales, branches spotted with light lenticels .... **Alder buckthorn** (page 96)

39 {

Leaf-stalks strongly compressed .... see **40**

Leaf-stalks round or almost round .... see **42**

40 {

Leaves almost circular, leaf-stalks long ....**Aspen** (pages 38–39)

Leaves diamond-shaped or triangular-ovate.... .... see **41**

41 {

Leaves large, triangular, often with 1 or 2 glands at leaf bases. Large tree with wide crown ....**Black Italian poplar** (page 42)

Leaves smaller, without glands at leaf bases. Pyramidal tree with narrow crown .... **Lombardy poplar** (pages 40–41)

42 {

Under-surfaces of leaves whitish .... see **43**

Under-surfaces of leaves not whitish (but eventually bluish-green).. see **44**

43 {

Leaves broad, cordate, with hairy leaf-stalks ... **Ontario poplar** (pages 42–43)

Leaves narrower, ovate, with smooth leaf-stalks ......**Oregon balsam poplar** (pages 42–43)

44 { Leaf bases oblique ....(Elms) see **45**

Leaf bases not oblique .... see **47**

45 { Upper-surfaces of leaves glabrous (applies only to leaves from crown region)........................ see **46**

Upper-surfaces of leaves rough-haired, leaves often with 3 points........................ .....**Wych elm** (page 62)

46 { Under-sides of leaves curly-haired (visible with lens), leaf veins not forked at margins, long flower and fruit stalks ....**Fluttering elm** (pages 62–63)

Under-sides of leaves almost glabrous, leaf veins often forked near margins, short flower and fruit stalks .... **Smooth-leaved elm** (pages 62–63)

47 { Leaves obliquely cordate ....(Limes) see **48**

Leaves not obliquely cordate........................ see **50**

48 { Under-surfaces of leaves bluish-green and glabrous .... **Small-leaved lime** (page 97)

Under-surfaces of leaves light green .... see **49**

49 { Leaves, leaf-stalks and young shoots downy...........**Large-leaved lime** (pages 98–99)

Leaves, leaf-stalks and young shoots glabrous or slightly hairy .... **Common lime** (pages 98–99)

50 { Trees or bushes with thorns (N.B. not all branches need to have thorns) .... see **51**

Trees or bushes without thorns........................ see **55**

51 { Thorns in groups of 3, leaves with bristle-toothed margins ....**Barberry** (page 64)

Thorns solitary, leaves not bristle-toothed .... see **52**

52 { Leaf-stalks half as long as leaf-blades, or longer .... see **53**

Leaf-stalks less than half as long as leaf-blades.. .... see **54**

53 { Leaf-blade oval to nearly circular, with a very short point. Red anthers ....**Wild pear** (page 74)

Leaf-blade ovate to broadly elliptical with a longer point. Yellow anthers................ ....**Crab apple** (page 74)

54 { Young shoots glabrous, often emerald-green ....**Cherry plum** (page 84)

Young shoots downy, brownish .... **Bullace** (page 81)

55 { Leaves approximately as long as broad......... .... see **56**

Length of leaves definitely exceeds breadth ... . see **58**

56
Leaves up to ½ in. long, almost circular. Quite a low bush ....Dwarf birch (page 51)

Leaves up to 2 in. long, rounded, with short point, white flowers .... St Lucie cherry (page 86)

Leaves larger .... see **57**

57
Leaves glabrous, dark green, broadly rounded or notched at apex .... Common alder (pages 52-53)

Leaves downy, green, somewhat shortly pointed. Glandular hairs on leaf-stalks .... Hazel (page 55)

58
Leaf-stalks or leaf-bases with glands.......... ...... see **59**

Leaf-stalks and leaf-bases without glands................ see **62**

59
Flowers and fruits in long racemes .... see **60**

Flowers and fruits not in long racemes, but in short clusters .... see **61**

60
Leaves shiny, somewhat leathery, finely serrated .... Rum cherry (page 86)

Leaves dull, wrinkled, more coarsely serrated .... Bird cherry (page 85)

61
Glands on leaf-stalks, under-surfaces of leaves downy, leaves doubly serrated ....Wild cherry (page 82)

Glands on leaf margins at leaf-bases, under-surfaces of leaves glabrous, leaves singly serrated . .Dwarf cherry (page 83)

62
Lateral veins of leaves very distinct and extended to leaf margins .... see **63**

Lateral veins of leaves less distinct and branched at leaf margins .... see **67**

63
Leaf-edges distantly sinuate-crenate, buds long, pointed .... Beech (pages 56-57)

Leaf-edges singly or doubly serrated .... see **64**

64
Under-surfaces of leaves grey to bluish-grey .... Grey alder (page 53)

Under-surfaces of leaves green .... see **65**

65
Leaves up to 5 in. long, finely and doubly ser-rated, 'pleated' ....Hornbeam (page 54)

Leaves up to 2½ in. long, ovate-diamond-shaped with short or long points .... see **66**

66
Young shoots hairy, leaves singly serrated..... ....Hairy birch (page 51)

Young shoots warty, leaves doubly serrated ....Warty birch (page 50)

67
Bush with many stems, leaves 1-1½ in. long, oval with pointed indentations .... Snowy mespilus (page 68)

Tree with narrow crown, leaves ½-4 in. long, ovate to obovate, acuminate, with rounded indentations .... Berlin poplar (pages 40-41)

1. YEW, *Taxus baccata.*

a. Spray with seed, Oct. *b.* Male flowers, March–April. *c.* Female flowers,
Mar–Apr. All ×1. *d.* Group of trees. *e.* 15th century archers with yew bows.

2. SILVER FIR, *Abies alba*.

a. Upper side of spray. *b.* Cone. *c.* Persistent axis of cone. *d.* Cone scale. All × ⅔.
e. Whole tree.

3. CAUCASIAN FIR,
Abies nordmanniana.

a. Upper side of shoot. *b.* Female flowers, May–June. *c.* Under side of shoot with male flower buds. All × ⅔. *d.* Detail of twig with needles × 1. *e.* Cone × ⅕. *f.* Old and young trees.

4f. Bark on
young stem.

4. NOBLE FIR, *Abies nobilis. a.* Upper side of shoot. *b.* Under side with
male flower buds. *c.* Cone scale. All × ⅔. *d.* Cones × 1/10. *e.* Form of tree.

5. GIANT FIR, *Abies grandis*. *a*. Upper side of shoot. *b*. Under side of shoot. Both × $\frac{2}{3}$. *c*. Cone × $\frac{1}{10}$. *d*. Bark. *e*. Group of trees.

6 a

6 b

6 c

6 g

6 d

6 e

6 f

7 a

7 c

7 d

7 b

6 h

6 g

6. NORWAY SPRUCE,

Picea abies. *a.* Spray with cone × ⅔.
b. Seed × 1. *c.* Twig with needles × 1.
d. Comb type. *e.* Brush type. *f.* North
Swedish type. *g.* Uses. *h.* Nun Moth,
Lymantria monacha.

7. WHITE SPRUCE,

Picea glauca. *a.* Spray with cones.
b. Under side of shoot. Both × ⅔.
c. Shoot with male flowers. *d.* With
female flower. Both × 1. *e.* White
spruce hedge.

7 e

24

8 *a*

8. SITKA SPRUCE,
Picea sitchensis.

a. Spray and cone. *b.* Upper and under
sides of shoot. All × 2/3. *c.* Trees.

8 *c*

8 *b*

9 *c*

10 a   10 b   10 c

9. DOUGLAS FIR,

Pseudotsuga taxifolia.

a. Spray with cone ×⅔. *b.* Detail of
twig with needles ×1. *c.* Whole tree.

10. WESTERN HEMLOCK,

Tsuga heterophylla.

a. Spray with cones ×⅔. *b.* Detail of
twig with needles ×1. *c.* Whole tree.

9 b   9 a

11 b

11 a

11 c

11 d

11 e

11 f

11 g

11. EUROPEAN LARCH,
Larix decidua.

a. Spray with *old* cones. *b.* Mature cone.
c. Annual shoot. *d.* Male flower. *e.* Female
flower, April–May. All × 1. *f.* Tree in
winter. *g.* Example of uses.

12. JAPANESE LARCH,
Larix leptolepis.

a. Twig with female flowers, May.
b. Part of twig with mature cone. *c.* Seed.
All × 1. *d.* Tree in winter.

12 b

12 c

12 a

12 d

13. SCOTS PINE,

Pinus sylvestris.

a. Shoot with male flowers, May–June. *b.* Shoot with female flowers and young cones. Both × 1. *c.* Central European type. *d.* North Swedish type. *e.* Use of pine logs. *f.* Pine Looper Moth, *Bupalus piniarius* × 1.

14 c

14 a

14 b

14. MOUNTAIN PINE, *Pinus mugo*.

a. Tip of shoot with young cone. *b.* Shoot with mature cone. Both × ⅔. *c.* Two different types of mountain pine (*left* the tall variety, *rostrata*).

15. AUSTRIAN PINE, *Pinus nigra* var. *austriaca*

a. Part of branch with cone × ⅔. *b.* Silhouette of branch × ¹⁄₁₀. *c.* Form of tree.

15 a

15 c

15 b

16 a

16 b

16 c

16. JACK PINE,
Pinus banksiana.

a. Shoot with young cones. b. Mature cone. Both × ⅔. c. Branch with cones in the middle of annual shoots × ⅛.

17. LODGEPOLE PINE,
Pinus contorta.

a. Shoot with young cones and buds. b. Needle fascicle and mature cone. c. Pine Shoot Moth, *Evetria buoliana.* All × ⅔. d. Branch with cones in middle of annual shoots. Last year's shoots attacked by Pine Shoot Moth × ⅛.

17 d

17 c

17 b

17 a

18. CEMBRAN PINE,
Pinus cembra.

a. Shoot. *b.* Needle fascicle. *c.* Mature
cone. *d.* Seed. All × ⅔. *e.* Form of tree.
f. Example of use of wood.

19. WEYMOUTH PINE, *Pinus strobus.*

a. Tip of shoot. *b.* Cone. *c.* Needle fascicle. All × $\frac{2}{3}$.
d. Silhouette of branches × $\frac{1}{12}$. *e.* Group of trees.

20 c

20 b

20 a

21 b   21 a

20. WESTERN RED CEDAR, *Thuja plicata.*

a. Spray with cone. *b.* Mature cone.
c. Seed. All × 1. *d.* Whole tree.

21. WHITE CEDAR, *Thuja occidentalis.*

a. Upper side of shoot. *b.* Mature cones. Both × 1. *c.* Whole tree.

20 d   21 c

22. LAWSON CYPRESS,
Chamaecyparis lawsoniana.

a. Male flowers. *b.* Young cones. *c.* Mature cones. Whole spray × 1. *d.* Young cones. *e.* Under side of branchlet. *d* and *e* × 5. *f.* Top of tree. *g.* Whole tree.

23. JUNIPER, *Juniperus communis.*

a. Shoot with ripe and unripe fruits (berry-like cones) × 1. *b.* Gall ('Whooping berry') × 1½. *c.* Shoot with ripe berries × 1½. *d.* Example of use. *e.* Form types.

22 g

22 a

22 b

22 c

22 f   *22 e*   *22 d*

23 b

23 c

23 d

23 e

23 a

MATURE CONES (×½)

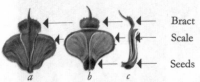

Bract
Scale
Seeds

Cone bract, scale and seeds of noble fir.
a. Outside. *b.* Inside. *c.* Side view.

SILVER FIR   CAUCASIAN FIR   NOBLE FIR

SCOTS PINE   MOUNTAIN PINE (3 types)   AUSTRIAN PINE

WHITE SPRUCE

SITKA SPRUCE

DOUGLAS FIR

WESTERN HEMLOCK

WESTERN RED CEDAR

WHITE CEDAR

LAWSON CYPRESS

NORWAY SPRUCE

GIANT FIR

EUROPEAN LARCH

JAPANESE LARCH

JACK PINE

LODGEPOLE PINE

CEMBRAN PINE

WEYMOUTH PINE

24 a

24 c

24 b

24 d

24 f

24. ASPEN, *Populus tremula.*

a. Shoot with leaves. *b.* Shoot with female catkins. *c.* Mature female catkins. *d.* Top of sucker. All × 1. *e.* Tree in winter. *f.* Wood used for matches.

25. WHITE POPLAR,
Populus alba.

a. Shoot with leaves showing upper and under sides. *b.* Top of sucker. *a* and *b* × 1. *c.* Tree in winter.

25 a

24 e   25 c   25 b

26 a

26 b

26. GREY POPLAR, *Populus canescens.*

a. Shoot with leaves. *b.* Top of sucker. *a* and *b* ×1.
c. Tree with leaves. *d.* Winter silhouette.

27. BERLIN POPLAR,
Populus berolinensis.

a. Shoot with leaves × ⅔. *b.* Form of whole tree.

28. LOMBARDY POPLAR,
Populus nigra var. *italica.*

a. Leaf shoot, with spiral gall on leaf stalk caused by
aphid *Pemphigus spirothecae* × ⅔. *b.* Tree form.

26

A   *B*

Leaves (× ⅓).

A. *Aspen*.
B. *White Poplar*.
C. *Grey Poplar*.
D. *Berlin Poplar*.
E. *Lombardy Poplar*.
F. *Black Italian Poplar*.
G. *Ontario Poplar*.
H. *Oregon Balsam Poplar*.

27 a

28 a

26 d

C   D   E   F   G   H

27 b   28 b

42

29 a

29 b

29. BLACK ITALIAN POPLAR,
Populus serotina.

a. Shoot with leaves ×⅔.
b. Twig with male catkins
×1. *c.* Leaf base with
glands ×5. *d.* Pollarded
tree.

29 c

30. ONTARIO POPLAR,
Populus candicans. a. Shoot with leaves ×⅔.
b. Female catkins ×1. *c.* Tree in winter.

31. OREGON BALSAM
POPLAR, *Populus trichocarpa.*
Shoot with leaves ×⅔.

29 d

30 a

30 b

31

30 c

32. GOAT WILLOW, SALLOW, *Salix caprea.*

a. Female catkins, April. *b.* Male catkins, April. *c.* Tip of shoot with leaves. All ×1. *d.* Tree in March.

34c. Bush in winter.

33. EARED WILLOW, *Salix aurita.* Shoot with leaves ×1.
34. GREY WILLOW, *Salix cinerea. a.* Male catkins ×1. *b.* Leaves ×1.

46

35. Creeping Willow

36. Caspian Willow

37. Common Osi

38. Crack Willow

39. White Willow

38 *a*

39 *a*

35. CREEPING WILLOW,

Salix repens. Twigs bearing catkins, April; shoot with leaves. Both × ⅔.

36. CASPIAN WILLOW,

Salix acutifolia. Male catkins, March; leaves, and twig with red bark. All × ⅔.

37. COMMON OSIER, *Salix viminalis*. End of shoot with leaves × ⅔.

38. CRACK WILLOW,

Salix fragilis. Tip of shoot with leaves; shoot with male catkins, May–June; twig which has put out roots. All × ⅔. *a*. Whole tree in winter.

39. WHITE WILLOW,

Salix alba. Tip of shoot with leaves, and twig with male catkins, May, × ⅔. *a*. Trees in winter: *left*, with normal branching; *right*, with pendulous branches.

Examples of the uses of willow.

40. BAY-LEAVED WILLOW, *Salix pentandra*.

a. Shoot with leaves and female catkin, May–June. *b*. Male catkin. *c*. Seed capsules almost ripe, Nov. All ×1. *d*. Tree in winter.

41. SWEET GALE, BOG MYRTLE,
Myrica gale.

a. Female catkin. *b*. Male catkins. *c*. Branch with leaves, from a male plant. All ×1.

42. WARTY BIRCH,
Betula pendula.

a. Spring shoot. Female catkin on left, male catkin on right.
b. Male catkin, July, which will produce pollen next spring.
c. Shoot with leaves and mature female catkin. All ×1.
d. Winged seed. e. Catkin scale. d, e ×4. f. Tree in winter.

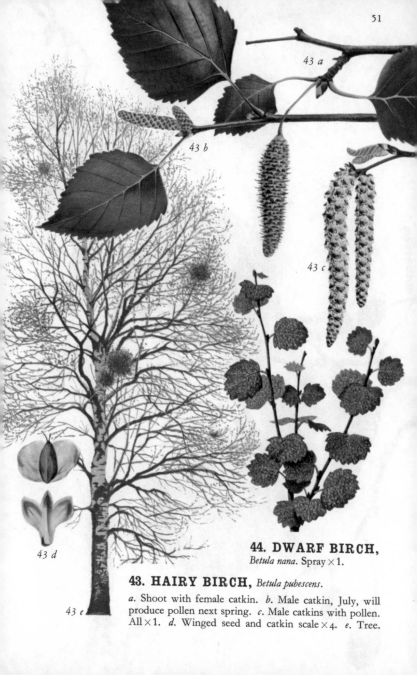

43 a

43 b

43 c

43 d

43 e

44. DWARF BIRCH,
Betula nana. Spray × 1.

43. HAIRY BIRCH, *Betula pubescens.*

a. Shoot with female catkin. *b.* Male catkin, July, will produce pollen next spring. *c.* Male catkins with pollen. All × 1. *d.* Winged seed and catkin scale × 4. *e.* Tree.

45 e

45 g

45 b

45 d

45 a

45 c

45 f

45. COMMON ALDER,
Alnus glutinosa.

a. Shoot with leaves and male catkins, Aug. *b.* Old female catkin. *c.* Female catkins, Aug. *d.* Male catkins with pollen, Mar. *e.* Female catkins in flower. All × ¾. *f.* Young trees. *g.* Old tree. *h.* Uses.

46. GREY ALDER, *Alnus incana.*

a. Shoot with leaves and male catkins, Sept. *b.* Female catkins, Sept. *c.* Old female catkins. All × ¾. *d.* Tree in winter.

45 h

46 b

46 d

46 a

46 c

47. HORNBEAM,

Carpinus betulus. *a*. Leaves and fruit cluster. *b*. Male catkins, May. *c*. Female catkin, May. All × ¾. *d*. Tree in winter. *e*. Cross-section of stem. *f*. Uses.

48. HAZEL, *Corylus avellana*.

a. Male catkins, February–April.
b. Female catkins, March–April.
c. Shoot with male catkins and nuts,
October. *d.* Nuts, wild and cultivated
forms. All×¾. *e.* Whole bush.

49. BEECH, *Fagus sylvatica*.

a. Long and short shoots with leaves × ⅔. *b*. Male
flower, May × ⅔. *c*. Female flower, May × ⅔. *d*. Fruit
× 1. *e*. Seedling × ⅔. *f*. Tree in winter. *g*. Tree in
summer. *h*. Examples of uses.

g   e   h

a

b

50. PEDUNCULATE OAK, *Quercus robur*.

a. Shoot with male catkins, May. *b*. Shoot with acorns and
leaves, with marble galls on one of the leaves. *a* and *b* ×1.
c. Tree in summer. *d*. Examples of uses.

51. SESSILE OAK,
Quercus petraea.

a. Shoot with leaves and acorns × ⅔. *b.* Trees in winter.

52. RED OAK,
Quercus borealis.

a. Leaves. *b.* Twig with two generations of acorns. *c.* Autumn colour. All × ⅔. *d.* Mature acorn with cup × 1. *e.* Initial stage of next year's acorn × 1. *f.* Bark. *g.* Tree in autumn.

53 a

53 c

53 b

53 d

53. WYCH ELM,
Ulmus glabra.

a. Shoot with leaves × ⅔. *b.* Shoot with inflorescences, March × 1. *c.* Fruit (winged nut) × 1. *d.* Tree in winter.

54. SMOOTH-LEAVED ELM, *Ulmus carpinifolia.*

a. Shoot with leaves × ⅔. *b.* Inflorescence, March × 1. *c.* Fruit × 1. *d.* Bud × 1. *e.* Tree in summer.

55. FLUTTERING ELM, *Ulmus laevis.*

a. Shoot with leaves × ⅔. *b.* Inflorescence, March × 1. *c.* Fruit × 1. *d.* Bud × 1. *e.* Tree in winter. Rest of the avenue is wych elm.

54 c

54 d

55 d

55 c

54 a

54 b

55 a

55 b

55 e

54 e

56. BARBERRY,
Berberis vulgaris.

a. Flowering shoot, May–June.
b. Branch with fruits (berries).
c. Upper and under side of leaf with black rust. *d.* Black rust on ear of corn. All × 1. *e.* Form of bush.

57. RED CURRANT,
Ribes rubrum.

above: Flowers and leaves, May.
below: Fruits (berries): All × 1.

58. BLACK CURRANT,
Ribes nigrum.

above: Flowers and leaves, May.
below: Fruits (berries). All × 1.

59 a

59 c

59 b

60 a

60 b

60 c

60 d

59. GOOSEBERRY,
Ribes uva-crispa.

a. Shoot with flowers, April.
b. Fruits. *c.* Magpie Moth,
Abraxis grossularia. All ×1.

60. ALPINE CURRANT,
Ribes alpinum.

a. Female flowers, May. *b.* Male
flowers. *c.* Leaves and berries.
d. Whitish buds, Oct. All ×1.

61. WILLOW-LEAVED SPIRAEA,
Spiraea salicifolia. Flowering shoot, June–July × ⅔.

62. SORBARIA,
Sorbaria sorbifolia. Inflorescence and leaf, June–July × ⅔.

63. COTONEASTER,
Cotoneaster integerrima. a. Flowering shoot, May. *b.* Shoot with fruits. Both × ⅔.

64 a

64 b

65 d

64. SNOWY MESPILUS,
Amelanchier spicata.

a. Flowering shoot, May. *b.* Fruit cluster and leaf, August–September. Both ×1.

65d. Silhouette of old hawthorn tree in winter.

65. MIDLAND HAWTHORN, *Crataegus oxyacanthoides*. *a*. Shoot with fruits (haws). *b*. Fruit in section (2 stones). *c*. Flowers, June. All ×1.

66. COMMON HAWTHORN, *Crataegus monogyna*. *a*. Flowers, May–June. *b*. Fruit, shown in section (1 stone). *c*. Shoot with fruits (haws). All ×1.

68 c

68 d

69 d

69 e

1   2   3

67

67. **MISTLETOE**, *Viscum album*.

68. **ROWAN**, *Sorbus aucuparia*.

a. Fruit cluster. *b.* Inflorescence, May–June.
Both ×⅔. *c.* Fruit (pome) ×1. *d.* Leaf ×¼.
e. Tree in winter.

69. **WHITEBEAM**,
Sorbus aria var. *rupicola*.

a. Flowers, May–June. *b.* Fruits, leaves and
buds. *c.* Cherry Fruit Moth, *Argyresthia con-
jugella.* All ×⅔. *d.* Fruit ×1. *e.* Leaf forms of
different varieties: 1. var. *obtusifolia,* 2. var.
typica, 3. var. *rupicola,* ×¼.

68 e

68 b

68 a

69 a

69 c

69 b

72

70 a

71 a

70. SWEDISH WHITEBEAM,

Sorbus intermedia. *a.* Shoot with leaves and fruits. *b.* Flowers, June. Both × ⅔. *c.* Fruit × 1. *d.* Use of wood.

71. FINNISH WHITEBEAM,

Sorbus hybrida. *a.* Shoot with leaves and fruits. *b.* Flowers, May–June. Both × ⅔. *c.* Fruit × 1.

72. WILD SERVICE TREE, *Sorbus torminalis.*

a. Shoot with leaves and fruits. *b.* Flowers, May–June. Both × ⅔. *c.* Fruit × 1.

70 b

70 d

71 b

72 b

0 c

1 c

2 c

72 a

73. CRAB APPLE,
Malus sylvestris.

a. Shoot with leaves and fruit.
b. Flowers, May. *c.* Dwarf shoots developed into thorns (false spines). All × 1.

74. WILD PEAR,
Pyrus communis.

a. Flowers, May. *b.* Leaves and fruit, October. Both × 1.

74

73 *a*

73 *c*

73 *b*

74 *a*

74 *b*

75. RASPBERRY,
Rubus idaeus.

a. Shoot with leaves and fruits.
b. Conical fruit core. *c.* Section
of detached fruit. *d.* Flowering
shoot, June. *e.* Dark Green Frit-
illary, *Argynnis aglaia.* All × ⅔.

76. BLACKBERRY,
Rubus fruticosus.
a. Leaf shoot (leaf with
5 leaflets). *b.* Flowering
shoot (leaves with 3 leaflets), June–Aug. *c.* Fruit
cluster. All × ⅔.

77. DEWBERRY,
Rubus caesius.

a. Shoot with fruit.
b. Shoot with leaves and
flowers, June – September. Both × ⅔.

78 *a*

79 *a*

78 *b*

78. DOG ROSE,
Rosa canina.

a. Shoot with leaves and flowers.
b. Hip. All × 1.

79. BURNET ROSE,
Rosa spinosissima.

a. Shoot with leaves and flowers.
b. Hip. All × 1.

79 *b*

81 *b*

80 b

80 a

81 a

80. RAMANAS ROSE,
Rosa rugosa.

a. Shoot with leaves and flowers.
b. Hip. All ×1.

81. SWEET BRIAR, EGLANTINE,
Rosa eglanteria.

a. Shoot with leaves and flowers.
b. Hip. All ×1.

82. BLACK-THORN, SLOE,
Prunus spinosa.

a. Shoot with leaves and fruits (drupes). *b.* Fruit stone. *c.* Flowers, April–May. All × 1. *d.* Branch with spines × ½. *e.* Hedge in flower.

83. BULLACE, *Prunus insititia*.

a. Twig in winter ×1. *b*. Flowering shoot, April–May ×1. *c*. Branch with leaves ×⅔. *d*. Fruit, Oct–Nov ×1. *e*. Fruit stone ×1.

84 e. Flowering tree

84. WILD CHERRY, GEAN, *Prunus avium*.

a. Flowering branch, May. *b*. Branch with fruits and leaves, July. *c* and *d*. Colour variations. All × ⅔.

85. DWARF CHERRY,
Prunus cerasus.

a. Shoot with leaves. *b.* Branch with fruits,
July–August. *c.* Shoot with flowers, May.
a, b and *c* × ⅔. *d.* Tree in winter.

86. CHERRY PLUM, *Prunus cerasifera*.

a. Flowering branches, April–May. *b.* Shoot with leaves and fruits. *c.* Section of fruit showing stone. All×⅔. *d.* Tree in winter.

87. BIRD CHERRY,

Prunus padus. *a.* Flower cluster, May.
b. Shoot with leaves and fruits, Sept.
c. Fruit stone. All ×1.

88 a

88. RUM CHERRY,
Prunus serotina.

a. Flower cluster, May. b. Fruits, October. c. Fruit stone. All × 1.

88 b   88 c

89. ST. LUCIE CHERRY, *Prunus mahaleb.*

a. Leaves and fruits × 1.

89 a   89 b. Used for pipes

90. ROBINIA, LOCUST, FALSE ACACIA,

Robinia pseudoacacia.

a. Flower cluster, June $\times \frac{2}{3}$. *b.* Pods, Sept $\times \frac{2}{3}$. *c.* Leaf $\times \frac{1}{3}$. *d.* Bark $\times \frac{1}{6}$. *e.* Tree in winter.

91 b   91 a   91 c

91. BROOM, *Sarothamnus scoparius.*

a. Shoot with leaves and flowers, May–June ×1. *b.* Shoot with pods, October ×1.
c. Bush in winter ×c. $\frac{1}{10}$.

92. GORSE, FURZE, WHIN.
Ulex europaeus.

a. Branch with flowers, April–June ×1.
b. Pod, August ×1. *c.* Whole bush × $\frac{1}{10}$.

92 *a*

92 *b*

92 *c*

93. HOLLY, *Ilex aquifolium*.

a. Shoot in winter × ⅔. *b*. Leaves from upper half of the tree × ⅔. *c*. Use of wood. *d*. Whole tree.

94. SPINDLE TREE,
Euonymus europaeus.

a. Shoot with leaves and fruits (capsules), September × ⅔. *b.* Shoot with flowers, May–June × ⅔.

95. NORWAY MAPLE, *Acer platanoides*.

a. Inflorescence, May–June. *b.* Leaves. *c.* Fruits (divided into 2 parts, each part a winged nut). All ×½. *d.* Autumn colour. *e.* Bark ×⅛. *f.* Trees in winter.

96.
SYCAMORE,   *Acer pseudoplatanus.*

a. Inflorescence and under side of leaf, May–June × ½.
b. Leaf and fruits × ½. *c.* Leaf tracery. *d.* Bark × ⅛.
e. Tree in winter. *f.* Example of use.

97. FIELD MAPLE,

Acer campestre. a. Flowers: *left*, male,
right, hermaphrodite, ×3. *b.* Inflorescence,
May–June ×1. *c.* Leaves and fruits ×1.
d. Bark with cork rib formation, also shown
in section, ×1. *e.* Tree in winter.

98. HORSE CHESTNUT,
Aesculus hippocastanum.

a. Part of inflorescence, May–June × 1. *b.* Leaf
× ½. *c.* Fruit (capsule and seed) × ⅔. *d.* Bud × 1.
e. Flowering tree. *f.* Tree in winter.

96

99 c

99 a

99 b

99 d

99. ALDER BUCKTHORN,
Frangula alnus.

a. Branch with leaves and fruits (drupes)
×¾. *b.* Twig with flower and bud, June
×2. *c.* Bush in winter. *d.* Use in manufacture of gunpowder.

100. PURGING BUCKTHORN,
Rhamnus catharticus.

100 a

100 b

100 c

100 d

a. Twig in winter with dwarf
shoots ×¾. *b.* Branch with leaves
and fruits (drupes) ×¾. *c.* Female
flower. *d.* Male flower. Both ×2.

101. SMALL-LEAVED LIME, *Tilia cordata.*

a. Flowering branch, July × ¾.
b. Branch with fruits, October × ¾.
c. Tree in winter.

98

102 *a*

102 *b*

103 *b*

103 *a*

103 d

103 c

102. LARGE-LEAVED LIME, *Tilia platyphyllos*.

a. Flowering branch, July.
b. Fruits. Both × ⅔.

103. COMMON LIME, *Tilia vulgaris*.

a. Shoot with leaves and flowers × ⅔. *b*. Fruits × ⅔. *c*. Trees in summer. *d*. Tree in winter.

104. MYRICARIA,
Myricaria germanica.

a. Inflorescence, July–August × 1.
b. Shoot with leaves × ⅔.

105. DAPHNE,
Daphne mezereum.

a. Flowering shoot, March. *b.* Shoot
with berries and leaves, July. Both × 1.

104 a

104 b

105 a

105 b

106. SEA BUCKTHORN,
Hippophaë rhamnoides.

a. Branch with male flowers, May.
b. Shoot with leaves and fruits,
September–October. Both × 1.

a

b

107. IVY, *Hedera helix.* *a.* Leaf shoot. *b.* Flowering shoot, October × ⅔.

a

108. WILD ROSEMARY, *Ledum palustre.* *a.* Inflorescence, June × ⅔.

109. DOGWOOD,
Cornus sanguinea.

a. Branch with leaves and fruits (drupes), Sept–Oct. *b.* Inflorescence, June–July. *c.* Leaf with autumn colour, Nov. All × 1.

110. ASH, *Fraxinus excelsior*.

a. Tree in summer. *b*. Tree in winter.
c. Branch with leaves and fruits
(winged nuts or 'keys'), August × ½.
d. Male flowers, April–May. *e*. Female flowers, April–May. *f*. Ripe
fruit. *d*, *e* and *f* × 1. *g*. Uses of wood.

c

d

f

e

111 a

111 c

111 b

112 a

112 b

113 a

113 b

111. LILAC,
Syringa vulgaris.

a. Shoot with inflorescence and leaves, May–June × 1. *b.* Fruits (capsules) × 1. *c.* Broad-bordered Bee Hawk Moth, *Haemorrhagia fuciformis.*

112. PRIVET,
Ligustrum vulgare.

a. Inflorescence, June–July. *b.* Shoot with fruits and leaves. Both × 1.

113. TEA TREE,
Lycium halimifolium.

a. Shoot with flowers and leaves, June – August × 1. *b.* Fruits (berries), September–October × 1. *c.* Silhouette of branches.

113 c

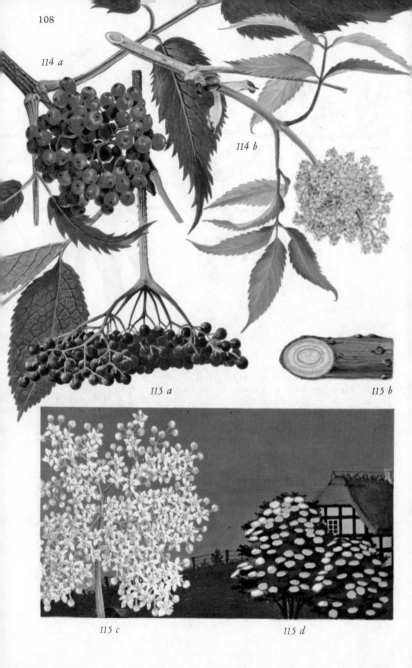

114 a

114 b

115 a

115 b

115 c

115 d

114. RED-BERRIED ELDER,

Sambucus racemosa. *a.* Fruit cluster (drupe),
July–Aug. *b.* Flowering shoot, April–May,
showing light brown pith. Both × ⅔.

115. COMMON ELDER,

Sambucus nigra. *a.* Fruit cluster, Sept–Oct.
b. Section of twig, showing pale pith. *c.* Part
of inflorescence, June–July, All × ⅔. *d.* Bush.

116. GUELDER ROSE, SNOWBALL TREE,

Viburnum opulus. *a.* Leaves and fruits (drupes).
b. Inflorescence, June. Both × ⅔.

116 a

116 b

117. SNOWBERRY,

Symphoricarpus racemosus. Leaves, flowers and fruits (berries), September × ⅔.

118 a

118 b

119

118. HONEYSUCKLE, WOODBINE,
Lonicera periclymenum.

a. Shoot with leaves and berries. b. Shoot with flowers, June–August. c. A young beech stem distorted by entwining honey-suckle. All × ⅔.

119. BLUE-BERRIED HONEYSUCKLE, *Lonicera coerulea.*

Twig with fruits and leaves × ⅔.

118 c

120. WOODY HONEYSUCKLE,
Lonicera xylosteum.

a. Shoot with flowers, May–June × 1.
b. Shoot with fruits (berries) × 1.

DESCRIPTIONS OF TREES AND BUSHES

The descriptive sections are arranged as follows:

First, notes on nomenclature, then a botanical description, followed by an account of the biology, habitat and utilization of the species. Finally, there is information on geographical distribution and, for the forest trees and some shrubs, a map to show the natural spread. A number of illustrations are included to explain botanical details. The heights of trees, and also their girths, are given—except where otherwise stated—in terms of the largest living British specimen. The Glossary (p. 220) and the keys (pp. 5–16), should be consulted for explanation of unfamiliar terms.

Yew Family, Taxaceae.

1. Yew, Taxus baccata

The English name 'yew' is derived from the Welsh *yw*. This in turn is related to the Gaelic *iubhar*, which is pronounced *ure* and often features, in that form, in Scottish place names. The Latin name *taxus* comes from the verb *texere*, to weave. The bast of yew has been used, like that of lime, for plaiting (braiding) and weaving.

Yew is the only representative of its family growing wild in Europe. It may be found as a tree up to 90 ft. tall, but is often only a thick bush 6–10 ft. high, with many stems which have not infrequently grown together so that the tree has the appearance of having a single stem; its girth may reach 34 ft.

The young bark is reddish-brown, but with age becomes greyish-brown and peels off in thin flakes. The needles are dark green and glossy on the upper-side, and light green and dull on the under-side. They are ribbed, and are soft and

blunt. The needles are up to 1 in. long and remain in position for several years. Like the majority of conifers, yew is an evergreen.

Yew is normally dioecious, i.e. the male and female flowers each occur on separate trees. There are, however, some individual trees that bear both male and female flowers.

The male flowers come from comparatively large globular buds, which are often found in great numbers; they arise on the under-side of the shoots and are most conspicuous.

The female flowers, which come from smaller ovoid buds at the end of very short shoots, contain one ovule. At the time of flowering this secretes a small, gummy drop to which the pollen from the male flowers sticks. When fruiting has taken place the ovule grows, becoming a large thick-skinned seed covered by a juicy seed cap, which is first green and later pinkish-red.

The wood is very hard and elastic, with a very narrow yellowish-white sapwood and a dark reddish-brown, naturally durable, heartwood. It is completely lacking in resin. Yew was formerly so highly valued for its wood that in the course of the centuries its frequency has been considerably reduced. A

 ←section

notable example in history of the use of yew is the long-bow, which was largely responsible for the English victory at Agincourt in 1415. Yew is also employed in ornamental carving and turnery.

A particular feature of yew foliage is that it is poisonous to animals, especially to horses. But ponies grazing around yew trees in the New Forest never suffer; apparently the poisonous principle is only developed when leaves are cut and left to wither. The bark and the seed are poisonous but the red pulp of the berry is harmless. Birds swallow, and spread, the seed without harm.

Yew is indigenous to central and southern Europe, Algeria, Asia Minor, the Caucasus and northern Spain. It grows wild in most parts of the British Isles. Its association with churchyards often dates from the congregations that met beneath its shade, before the first parish church was built.

Pine Family, *Pinaceae*.

2. Silver Fir, *Abies alba*

The name 'silver fir' is a translation from the German *Weisstanne*, which refers to the two white stripes on the under-sides of the needles.

European silver fir reaches a height of 150 or even 180 ft., with girths of up to 23 ft. It is distinguished by the flat, spread-out branches with very short needles ($\frac{1}{2}$ to 1 in. long), which are green and have two white stripes on the under-sides. The

section ⟶

needles are thick and are notched at the apex, and the buds do not have the covering of resin so general in many other firs of this *Abies* genus.

As in many conifers, the branches are arranged in regular whorls, and each intervening space represents a year's growth. If all the whorls of a tree can be seen one can easily tell its age.

Male and female flowers are placed separately on silver fir. The short catkin-like male flowers are found on the previous year's shoot, often in considerable numbers. The upright female flowers occur singly near the tip of the previous year's shoot.

The cones, like those of all *Abies* firs, are erect, and when ripe they disintegrate into seeds, cone scales and bracts. Only the persistent axis remains on the tree. The cylindrical brownish cones are up to 6 in. long, and the bracts project, with a narrow reflexed tip.

Silver fir, which is indigenous to southern and central Europe, was introduced to Britain early in the seventeenth century. However, since 1920 it has suffered so severely from a tiny aphis, *Adelges piceae*, which does serious harm in Britain though not on the Continent, that it is now seldom planted.

The wood is soft and light, free

from resin, and greyish-white; the heartwood is colourless. It is used as building timber, for the interior parts of furniture, and also for box-making, and much is still imported.

free, keep their branches right down to the ground, a feature which makes it very suitable for parks. In Britain it is rarely found outside ornamental grounds, where it grows up to 120 ft. tall.

The wood is used as building timber and does not differ greatly from that of silver fir.

3. Caucasian Fir,
Abies nordmanniana

The Latin name of this tree was given in honour of the Finnish botanist A. von Nordmann, who was Professor of Botany in Odessa and discovered the tree in the Caucasus in 1836. It also grows in the Crimea.

Caucasian fir differs from silver fir in its glossy dark green needles, which spread upwards and forwards. This arrangement of needles means that the shoots form a round or half-round shape, with a clear 'parting' on the under-side. The needles, which are about $\frac{1}{2}$ in. long, have two white stripes on the under-sides and a notch at the apex.

The male and female flowers are placed in the same way as in the silver fir, but the cones are more cylindrical and rounded.

A characteristic of Caucasian fir is that even old trees, if they stand

4. Noble Fir,
Abies nobilis (Abies procera)

The English and Latin names of this tree arise from its appearance.

Noble fir is easily recognized, as its flat bluish-grey to bluish-green needles are the same on each side and, unlike the preceding species, do not have two white stripes on the underside. The needles, which are about $\frac{1}{2}$ in. long, are placed very close together, and on the under-sides of the branches are curved and spread

outwards, forming a typical 'parting'. On the upper-sides of the shoots the needles curve upwards.

The young shoots are covered with short reddish-brown hair.

Another special characteristic is that the cones are up to 10 in. long and 3 in. wide. The ends of the bracts are prominent and reflexed, and almost cover the cone scales. These large cones are very heavy, and on account of their weight they sometimes 'capsize', failing to maintain the typically upright position of the *Abies* firs.

The bark is light grey, like elephant hide, and there are always resin blisters on young stems.

Noble fir comes from Oregon in western North America and was introduced to Europe in about 1830, as a park tree. Like many other species which were originally specimen trees it has also become a forest tree, and its branches are much appreciated as green decoration.

The wood of noble fir differs very little from that of the other silver firs. The tree is being planted on a small scale for its timber, particularly in the west of Scotland and in Ireland. In Britain, it reaches heights up to 148 ft.

Giant fir has flat shoots with long needles (up to 2¼ in.) which are bright green above and have two white stripes on their under-sides. The buds are coated with resin and thus differ from the European silver fir already described. Giant fir can also be recognized by the fact that the bark has characteristic blisters containing aromatic resin. The cones are small, up to 4 in. long, with concealed bracts.

A species closely related to giant fir is the Colorado fir, *Abies concolor*, which, on account of its excellent growth and attractive bluish colour, is more suitable for gardens and parks. Its needles are a dull greyish-green to bluish-green on both sides, spaced quite far apart, and are usually curved upwards and outwards. Both these species of *Abies* and their intermediate forms (*Abies concolor* var. *lowiana* with grey needles and flat shoots, etc.) grow in western North America; giant fir both on the coast and inland, *Abies concolor* further south and exclusively inland. These two trees were introduced to Europe in the middle of the nineteenth century.

5. Giant Fir, *Abies grandis*

Both the English and the Latin names of this tree express its great size.

Giant fir is well named, for in its native country trees can be found with heights up to 300 ft. In Britain it has shown remarkably fast growth.

A tree at Leighton Hall near Welshpool is 168 ft. tall; another at Inveraray in Argyll is 18 ft. round.

The wood, which is soft and light, is very suitable for use in the building industry and for various forms of joinery work. In North America the wood of giant fir is used to a considerable extent in the production of paper. Giant fir is being planted for timber production in Britain, but only on a small scale.

6. Norway Spruce, *Picea abies*

The name 'spruce' is an old word for Prussia, from which country the tree and its products 'spruce beer' (flavoured with needles) and 'spruce leather' (tanned with bark) were introduced to Britain. It is called Norway spruce to distinguish it from other trees of the genus *Picea*. It is also called 'spruce fir'.

This most important timber-producing tree is recognized by the green (not bluish-green) needles, with a more or less diamond-shaped

section

cross-section. The needles are identical on all four sides. The young branches are yellowish-brown, glabrous or slightly hairy.

Flowering takes place in May. The female flowers are a handsome red, but the colour is not so pronounced as in the silver fir. They are found mainly in the upper part of the crown, while the male flowers, which at first are also red, grow in the middle and the lower part of the crown. On any one tree the female flowers normally come out first, so that they are covered with pollen from other spruce trees before the male flowers of their own tree open.

In this way self-pollination and the consequent undesirable inbreeding is avoided. The male flowers produce pollen in such quantities that the ground under and near a spruce stand may be quite yellow. Similarly wind-borne pollen often lands on lakes and covers the surface of the water with a yellow layer. This phenomenon is often called 'sulphur rain' and can also be seen near male flowers of Scots pine.

Before pollination the female flower is upright; afterwards it bends down, and the fully developed cone is therefore pendulous. The cones, which may vary somewhat in length and thickness, are up to 3 in. long, with leathery, rounded cone scales.

The branches are arranged in whorls on the stem, but between each whorl there are often smaller side branches. A spruce board can thus be distinguished from a Scots pine board because between the large knots there are several small ones. Scots pine does not produce side branches on the annual shoot, and therefore has only large knots.

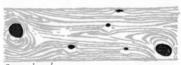
Spruce board

Scots pine board

The branching habit varies greatly in Norway spruce; there are many different form types and we shall describe some of the most typical. In some mountain districts of Scandinavia there is often the slow-growing *Nordland* or highland type, which is resistant to snow and wind.

It has a slender and narrow crown composed of horizontally projecting branches. Another mountain form is called the columnar type, which also has a narrow crown, but has pendulous branches. The lowland type, which is windfirm but less resistant to snow, is broader, fast growing, and has side branches level with the main branches. A fourth type is the 'comb spruce' with pendulous side branches, resembling those of mountain forms. There are other form types, for example snake type, whip type, conical, plate and pyramid types, which are often seen in gardens and parks, but have no significance in forestry.

The root system of Norway spruce is very shallow and therefore stands of this species are liable to wind-throw, especially if the soil becomes waterlogged. Attention to drainage is therefore important in spruce plantations.

Norway spruce and its varieties are indigenous to northern and central Europe and western Asia. It is not native in Britain, but was introduced in about 1548 and since then has been used to an increasing extent as a forest tree, reaching heights up to 156 ft.

In Continental forests the larvae of the nun moth, *Lymantria monacha*, may cause extensive damage by completely defoliating trees. In Britain there has only been damage on a small scale.

As Norway spruce both gives and tolerates a certain amount of shade, it is dark inside a spruce forest. This has a great effect on the ground vegetation under Norway spruce. In young stands with close canopy it is too dark for any vegetation, but when the plantation is older and the trees, as a result of thinning, stand less closely, enough light comes in to allow mosses and certain herbs

to grow. Very few flowering herbs are found and only occasionally is there an undergrowth of bushes.

Norway spruce wood has many uses in the building industry and in joinery. It is also used for box-making, piles, poles for power lines, chipboard, paper pulp and fuel.

7. White Spruce, *Picea glauca*

The 'white' in the name of this tree refers to the needles which, even if they are not white, are grey or bluish-green. The light colouring is due to a wax covering, especially round the many stomata.

This spruce differs from Norway spruce in having bluish-green to bluish-grey needles, the cross-section of which is four-sided and not

so flat. The young branches are greyish-yellow. The cones, which are green when young, and later a light brown, are often found in large numbers, and are as small as 1–2 in. long. If the needles are crushed they have a characteristic and strong

smell. Never a big tree, it only reaches heights around 75 ft.

White spruce is found across the north of North America and was introduced into Europe in about 1700.

White spruce is hardly ever planted as a timber tree as it grows too slowly and therefore does not reach sufficient dimensions. Though often tried in Britain, it has seldom given satisfactory results.

The wood resembles that of Norway spruce and if the quality is good, which it seldom is in Europe, it can be used for the same purposes. In America it is widely used for paper pulp.

8. Sitka Spruce, *Picea sitchensis*

Sitka is the name of a port in southern Alaska. The name 'Sitka' spruce refers to the fact that the tree was first recognized there.

Sitka spruce differs from the two previously described spruces (Nos. 6 and 7), in that it has flat needles, which on their upturned sides are green, and their under-surfaces whitish-blue. The needles are very sharp. The cones also differ; the scales are light brown, loosely adjacent, thinner and somewhat wavy. The cones are up to 3 in. long.

The bark is characteristic in that it peels off in rounded flakes. Another feature of Sitka spruce is that small shoots (epicormic branches) grow out of the otherwise branchless part of the stem of older trees, especially those which are in an open situation.

This species, which comes from North America's west coast, was introduced to Europe in about 1830 and since then has become an important forest tree both in Britain and also in Denmark. Sitka spruce is fast growing and produces excellent timber; it does particularly well on grassy uplands in the north and west, and some thirty million Sitka spruce are planted annually. It is not resistant to night frosts in the spring, and therefore should not be planted in hollows. It is windfirm and is often used for shelter-belts. In Britain it grows up to 160 ft. tall.

The wood is very light and tough, and is an excellent timber for building, joinery, box-making, chipboard and paper pulp. Among its special uses may be mentioned oars and aeroplane construction.

8a. Blue Spruce, *Picea pungens*

The name 'blue spruce' is most suitable for those types which are grown in gardens on account of their beautiful bluish-green needles. Other forms, which are not commonly grown in Britain, have dark green needles. The tree has also been called 'Colorado spruce' after its native country.

Both this and the next species of spruce (No. 8b) have, like the Sitka spruce, loose cones with thin wavy cone scales; but there the similarity

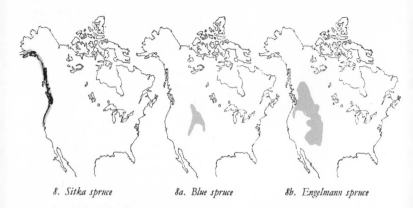

8. *Sitka spruce*　　　8a. *Blue spruce*　　　8b. *Engelmann spruce*

ends. Blue spruce has pure green to bright bluish-green needles, which are the same on all four sides, and have a sharp thorn-like apex. The young branches are smooth and yellowish-brown.

It is native in the Rocky Mountains (eastern Utah and Colorado) and is frequently used in British parks and gardens, but only reaches heights around 44 ft. It is usually the blue-needled form which one sees here.

8b. Engelmann Spruce,
Picea engelmanni

The English name is taken from the Latin name of the tree, given to it by the American botanist Parry in honour of his somewhat earlier colleague, G. Engelmann.

Engelmann spruce closely resembles blue spruce, but the needles are softer and not nearly so sharp. The young branches are a dull greyish-green, and have short glandular hairs. The cones are reddish-brown.

The tree grows wild in the mountains of western North America and was introduced into Europe in 1863. As a forest tree it is very little used, but has been planted experimentally, particularly in Norway. It grows up to 42 ft. tall.

9. Douglas Fir,
Pseudotsuga taxifolia

Douglas fir is named after the Scottish gardener David Douglas, who in 1827 introduced the tree to Europe.

Douglas fir has some superficial resemblance to silver fir, but the fresh-green soft needles lack white stripes on the under-sides, and the buds are thin and pointed and are

reminiscent of beech buds. The cones are pendulous and eventually fall off complete and unbroken. The bracts are very characteristic with their three-lobed points, and project far out between the cone scales.

The bark in youth is smooth, and has many resin blisters. With age Douglas fir develops a characteristic crusty bark, deeply fissured.

It is native on the west side of North America and grows best in the coastal districts, where it has reached a measured height of 417 ft. Further inland it changes gradually to a slightly different form with greyish-green needles, called grey Douglas fir, *Pseudotsuga taxifolia* var. *caesia*. Finally inland there is found, further to the south, the blue or Colorado Douglas fir, *Pseudotsuga glauca*, which has bluish-grey needles and smaller cones with much longer bracts. This last form is often found in Britain planted in gardens and

parks where it flourishes, but grows slowly.

In our woods we plant almost exclusively the 'green' Douglas fir, which grows faster and is less susceptible to the fungus diseases which attack both blue and grey Douglas. The tallest tree in Britain is a Douglas fir at Powis Castle, near Welshpool, 181 ft. high.

Douglas fir timber is similar to that of pine, with yellowish-white sapwood and reddish-brown heartwood. Good quality wood is especially sought after for house- and ship-building, joinery, box-making, plywood, ladder poles, and many other exacting uses, including hardboard and paper pulp.

10. Western Hemlock, *Tsuga heterophylla*

The early American settlers called this tree 'hemlock' as the needles, when crushed, smell like the umbelliferous plant which bore that name in England.

This conifer, which grows up to 146 ft. tall, has a pyramidal form with an extremely pendulous leading shoot. The needles are short,

with two light stripes on the undersides. The pendulous cones are small and stalkless. The bracts are hidden, and the cone scales are dark below and light above. The winter buds are plump. As the side branches are irregularly spaced throughout each year's growth, the tree has no definite whorls or storeys.

A nearly related species, *Tsuga canadensis*, is grown in gardens and parks, but here in Europe it nearly always has a wide crown and is a bushy tree with many stems. It has pointed winter buds and cones on short stalks, which serve to distinguish it.

Western hemlock grows wild from California to southern Alaska, and forms an important part of the Douglas fir and western red cedar forests where it flourishes even in very heavy shade. It is being planted on an increasing scale in Britain, because it yields a high volume of useful timber on ground of moderate fertility. It thrives on most former woodland sites, and is useful for underplanting or filling in gaps in open woods.

The timber, which has no distinct heartwood, is used for joinery and pulpwood in North America.

11. European Larch, *Larix decidua*

The English name 'larch', like the Danish name *Laerk*, comes from a dialect form of the German *Lärche*, which goes back to the Latin *larix;* but we do not know the origin of that name. In Welsh it is represented by *llarwydd*, and in Gaelic by *learach*.

The larch species differ from the other conifers described here, in that they are deciduous. They bear needles on two types of shoot—singly on long shoots at branch tips, and in clusters on short shoots further back.

European larch has greyish-yellow annual shoots, with fresh-green needles which are about 1 in. long, flat, and diamond-shaped in section.

Flowering takes place at the end of April. The male flowers grow on needle-less dwarf shoots, while the female flowers, whose bracts are usually a handsome red colour, grow on a dwarf shoot which bears needles. The cone scales are, at the time of flowering, very small, and green to pale reddish in colour. The mature cone is light brown, $1-1\frac{1}{2}$ in. long and $\frac{1}{2}-\frac{3}{4}$ in. wide. The thin cone scales are fairly closely spaced and the edges are not wavy. The bracts are the same colour as the cone scales, and are partly visible.

European larch is native to Europe, but as a wild tree is only common in the Alps, the Carpathians, and the Sudeten mountains. It was introduced in about 1620 and has since been frequently grown as a forest and park tree. It grows up to 145 ft. tall.

European larch is, however, threatened by a serious danger as it is susceptible to larch canker, a disease caused by a fungus which produces sores and swellings on the branches and stems, and may even kill the tree.

However, not all types of European larch are attacked with equal severity, and in various parts of Scotland there are now many very fine plantations, such as those of the Atholl estates in Perthshire. Certain Scottish strains resist the attacks of canker.

The timber has a yellowish-white, usually narrow sapwood, and a reddish-brown, naturally durable heartwood. Really good, straight stems of larch are very valuable, and their uses include masts of boats and ships and, as sawn timber, hull and deck planks. In addition, larch timber is used in the building and mining industries.

12. Japanese Larch,
Larix leptolepis

The name 'Japanese larch' refers to the native country of the tree.

The shoots of Japanese larch are a light reddish-violet colour, often tinged with blue, and have bluish-green needles about 1¼ in. long. The cones are ¾–1¼ in. long; the edges of the scales are wavy and bent outwards, which gives the cones a very typical rosette appearance.

This larch was originally indigenous to inner Hondo, but grows in northern and southern Japan. It was introduced to Britain as late as 1861, and has reached heights up to 105 ft.

Unlike European larch, Japanese larch is resistant to larch canker, and many foresters think it advisable to concentrate on growing this kind exclusively.

On the one hand we have a larch susceptible to canker, but often with good form; and on the other hand is a canker-resistant larch which is less well shaped, or at least bears coarse branches. By crossing the two species it is possible to get a progeny which possesses the best of the parents' characteristics; the individuals thus produced have a better form and finer branches than Japanese larch and are resistant to canker. In addition, these progenies are faster growing than the parent trees. This hybrid larch (*Larix eurolepis*) first arose accidentally on the Atholl estate at Dunkeld in Perthshire in about 1905. It is now increased deliberately by planned tree breeding.

13. Scots Pine, *Pinus sylvestris*

The name 'pine', from the Latin *pinus*, is used by botanists and foresters to distinguish this tree from other conifers, since its original name of 'fir' has been loosely applied to conifers of all kinds. It is called 'Scots' pine to distinguish it from other, introduced, pines. It is native to nearly all of Europe, including most of Britain, but as a wild tree we know it best in Scotland.

The original name, both for tree and timber, was simply 'fir', and this is still widely used. It comes from Anglo-Saxon *fyre* and Norse *furu* (Old Norse *fyri*) and is related to Danish *Fyr* and German *Föhre*. The Gaelic name is *guithais*. The Welsh for fir is *ffynidwydd*.

The Scots pine is an extremely important forest tree right across northern Europe. It has two bluish-green needles in each bundle. The needles grow, as in all pine trees, on dwarf shoots in the axils of the scale-leaves on the long shoot and are, at the base, enclosed in a sheath or needle-case. Solitary needles are only found on seedlings.

In May the male flowers produce pollen. These flowers are situated at the base of the long shoot, which is where a dwarf shoot with needles would otherwise appear. When the male flowers have dispersed their vast quantities of pollen they die and fall off, leaving a bare patch on the shoot. The female flowers at the end of the annual shoots are red and the size of small peas. They turn upwards at the time of pollination, but after this they bend downwards. About one year after pollination, fruiting takes place, and the cone first begins to grow in earnest. At the end of this second year in the cone's life the seeds are almost mature, and at the beginning of the third year they fall out during dry spring weather and are dispersed.

The mature cones are greyish-brown to yellowish-brown and hang on a short bent stalk. Each cone scale usually has a flat upper surface or apophysis with a central knob or umbo, and the lower part is thinner and darkish-brown in colour. The boundary between the thin part of the cone scale and the upper surface is light brown.

In youth the branches of Scots pine are arranged in whorls; there are no side branches on the actual annual shoot (as, for example, in

Norway spruce), but only at the extremities. With age the main axis of the tree is broken up, and the tree develops its characteristic crown. As in the Norway spruce, there are several different form types of Scots pine. The two most important are the North Scandinavian type with an elongated, and in older trees pointed, crown, and the central European type with the broad, short crown.

The bark of older Scots pine is thick and scaly at the base of the tree, dark reddish-brown to blackish-brown. Higher up it remains thinner and is bright reddish-yellow, peeling off in papery flakes. The inner bark was once eaten, in times of food scarcity.

The root system of Scots pine is usually robust, with a long, powerful taproot and strong, far reaching side roots. Scots pine is therefore resistant to wind-throw. It reaches heights up to 120 ft., and girths up to 18 ft.

Scots pine is a light-demander and also casts very little shade. Therefore pinewoods are open and light and, on the better soils, have a rich flora in which grasses predominate; often there is an undergrowth of various bushes.

Scots pine is sometimes attacked by the pine looper moth, *Bupalus piniarius*, whose larvae are liable to damage middle-aged stands and may, by defoliation, cause the death of trees. There have been few bad outbreaks in Britain, but in other countries, particularly Germany, the pine looper moth has caused serious damage.

The wood has a bright reddish-brown heartwood and a wide yellowish-white sapwood. Its uses are many, and well grown, close-ringed pine timber, free of dead knots, is much in demand. Scots pine from the eastern Scottish Highlands fulfils all these requirements, and for a long time has had a reputation for good quality.

Scots pine timber, which is also known in the trade as red deal or Baltic redwood, is our standard softwood for building, railway sleepers, telegraph poles, pit props, fencing, and heavy case-making, and much is also used for chipboard, hardboard, and paper pulp.

14. Mountain Pine, *Pinus mugo*

Mountain pine, as the name suggests, is, in a natural state, confined to mountain districts. It is grown mainly in gardens and is sometimes called dwarf pine.

Like Scots pine, mountain pine has two needles in each bundle, but these needles are pure green, not bluish-green. The cones are sessile and project horizontally, and the

scales have glossy brown upper surfaces, the form of which varies considerably (see illustration, p. 36). This pine occurs most frequently as a bush or multi-stemmed tree, and the lower part of the trunks are somewhat crooked.

A variety which grows in the French Alps and Pyrenees and is called Pyrenean or French mountain pine (*Pinus mugo* var. *rostrata*), has a single and straight stem up to 75 ft. tall. Other distinguishing features of this variety are that the cones are extremely oblique and the upper

surfaces of the scales have reflexed hooks on the outer sides.

Mountain pine comes from the mountains of central Europe, and is only planted for shelter in Britain.

The wood, which is usually far from straight, has broad pale sapwood and narrow dark brown heartwood. Firewood is practically its only use. Ethereal oils, which are used in various bath salts, are obtained from the needles.

15. Austrian Pine,
Pinus nigra var. *austriaca*

This is the Austro-Hungarian race of the variable European species *Pinus nigra*, the general distribution of which is shown in the map. This species is also called the 'black pine', from the Latin name, based on the French *pin noir;* this derives from the dark grey colour of the bark, which contrasts with the red bark of the Scots pine, or *pin rouge.*

This pine has dark green, closely-spaced needles which are 4–6 in. long. The cones are larger than those of the Scots pine, and always oblique or one-sided. The scales are wider and have a greyish-yellow upper surface and a reddish-yellow intermediate zone; the lowest part is dark violet.

Austrian pine is a tall, impressive tree, with dark grey rugged bark, and is therefore much planted in gardens and parks. As a forest tree it is no longer planted, because its form is too rough and branchy. But it is unequalled as a shelter-belt tree for regions of low rainfall. It grows well under extreme exposure near the sea, or on high chalk downs or limestone hills. It grows up to 120 ft. tall.

The home of this race is Austria and Hungary, but other races are found in southern Europe and elsewhere. One of these, Corsican pine, *Pinus nigra* var. *calabrica*, has lighter, softer and less closely-spaced needles, always somewhat twisted, and lighter-coloured bark. Corsican pine has proved a valuable timber producer in the south, east and Midlands of England, and also along the east coast of Scotland. It grows on sterile sands and heavy clays, but must have much sun and a low rainfall. A useful tree for fixing sand dunes. On good ground it reaches 135 ft. tall.

16. Jack Pine, *Pinus banksiana*

The name 'jack' signifies half-sized, from the tree's poor form and low stature. The Latin name commemorates the famous botanist Sir Joseph Banks, who discovered the tree in Labrador in 1766.

Jack pine is an irregularly-branched tree with somewhat twisted light green needles 1–2 in. long. Like lodgepole pine, it differs from the other two-needled pines in that it often bears cones both at the end and in the middle of the shoot.

The cones, which have a distinctly flattened prickle on the cone scale, are light greyish-brown and very twisted, almost distorted. Another characteristic is that the cones may remain on the tree for many years without opening, as most types need considerable heat to open them. In the north of North America, which is the home of this species, many of the cones open as a result of forest fires and thus the seed of jack pine is among the first to spread over a burnt area. This seed quickly germinates and re-afforests these areas. Pines with this type of cone are called, in America, close-pines.

In youth jack pine is a very fast-growing species and is tolerant and hardy; in America it is therefore planted to some extent on exposed sites. Its wood is used for coarse joinery and paper pulp. It grows up to 56 ft. tall.

17. Lodgepole Pine, *Pinus contorta*

The name 'lodgepole pine' occurred because the straight, strong, and light stems were chosen by the Red Indians for the poles of their lodges or wigwams. The Latin specific name *contorta* refers to the slight twist often found in the needles.

Lodgepole pine is a variable tree found along the coast, and amid the inland mountains, of western North America. Some of the coastal races are of poor form, little better than bushes, and therefore inland races, which are tall erect trees, were the first to be planted in Britain. As these proved ill-adapted to our climate, seed is now obtained from selected coastal races of good tree form.

Lodgepole pine has recently come into prominence as an important tree for the afforestation of difficult peaty moorland in Ireland, Scotland, northern England and Wales; over fifteen million trees are planted annually by the Forestry Commission. It yields a reasonably strong, workable timber, used in America in large quantities for joinery, box-making, and paper pulp, and it grows to a fair size, up to 102 ft.

Lodgepole pine differs from Scots pine in its darker green needles, which are 1–2 in. long. Its bark is distinctive, being dark grey, and

coastal forms

inland forms

generally smooth, but breaking off in fine flakes; it resembles the bark of the bird cherry (*Prunus padus*, No. 87). The cones are narrow and somewhat oblique, and bear a small sharp prickle on the centre of each scale.

18. Cembran Pine, *Pinus cembra*

'Cembran' comes from the Italian name *cembra*, which is possibly related to the German name *Zirbel*; *Zirbel* means 'whirl' and refers to the whorled structure of the cone; cf. the Latin name for a cone, *strobilus*, derived from a Greek word meaning to turn round or whirl.

Unlike all the species of pine previously described, cembran pine has five needles in each cluster. The

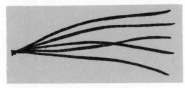

needles, which are dark green, closely placed and rigid, are 2–5 in. long and $\frac{1}{16}$ in. wide. They have a triangular cross-section. The young shoots are covered with dense brown-coloured down.

The cones are short (2–3 in. long), oval, and thick (1–2 in. across). When ripe they are light brown and contain large wingless seeds which are edible and have a pleasant taste.

Cembran pine grows into a tree up to 72 ft. tall, and when old has a large roundish crown. When the tree is isolated it keeps its long branches down to the ground.

The wood has light sapwood and light reddish-brown heartwood; it is very light and rarely breaks. It is the favourite wood of the famous

Swiss and Tyrolean wood carvers. In addition the timber is used for panels, furniture and other purposes, but as a result of the large consumption and the lack of new plantations, it is difficult to obtain in sufficient quantities.

In Britain the cembran pine may be seen in parks and gardens. It has been experimentally planted as a forest tree, but grows only slowly.

The natural distribution of this tree covers small regions in the Alps and Carpathians, and large areas in north-east Russia and northern Asia.

19. Weymouth Pine,
Pinus strobus

Weymouth pine was named after the landowner, Lord Weymouth, who first used this tree on a large scale in England when he planted his estate at Longleat in Wiltshire at the beginning of the eighteenth century. In North America it is known as 'white pine'.

Weymouth pine is another five-needled pine. The needles, which are fine, bluish-green and shiny, are 2–5 in. long and about $\frac{1}{2}$ mm. wide. The cross-section is triangular. The young shoots, which are at first green and later brownish, are somewhat hairy. The cones, which are very characteristic, are 4–6 in. long, slender and pendulous and have rather thin, loosely adjacent, scales. They are sold for decorations as 'banana cones'.

The bark on the trunk remains smooth and olive-brown for a considerable time, but later becomes fissured and grey.

In the north-east region of North America, Weymouth pine reaches heights of up to 150 ft. It would be a valuable forest tree in Europe if it were not so susceptible to attack by a fungus, the Weymouth pine blister rust, *Cronartium ribicola*. Planting has had to be abandoned until races which are resistant to this infection can be found.

Weymouth pine has whitish-yellow sapwood and yellowish-red heartwood. It is light and soft and has many special uses, such as pattern making for engineering.

Cypress Family, Cupressaceae.

20. Western Red Cedar,
Thuja plicata

The name 'cedar' comes from the Latin *cedrus*, which was originally applied to an Italian juniper. Later, it was used for many kinds of evergreen trees with fragrant foliage or timber, including the cedars of Lebanon referred to in the Bible. The early settlers gave the name

'cedar' to trees of the *Thuja* genus which they found in North America, supposing them to be these Biblical cedars. This species is called 'western' because it grows only in the westerly region, and 'red' from the colour of the bark. (For '*Thuja*', see No. 21.)

In dealing with western red cedar we come to a new family of conifers, namely the Cypress family, which includes the *Thuja* and *Chamaecyparis* species. These trees have scale-like leaves, and only seedlings and juvenile forms have needles. The cones are small, and the fruit leaves are not divided into bracts and scales.

The branchlets are very flat, regular and feathery. On the upper-sides they are a fresh dark green, and underneath they have fairly clearly defined greyish-green areas. On each leaf there is usually an indistinct gland.

Male and female flowers are produced on the same tree at the end of short branches. The oblong cones, which are about $\frac{1}{2}$ in. long, have a few (10–12) overlapping scales. The leading shoot is upright, and free-standing trees have a handsome pyramidal form.

Western red cedar is native to western North America and was introduced into Europe in 1853. It is frequently planted in parks, and as a forest tree is used mainly on the less exposed sites. It grows up to 129 ft. tall.

The wood is of high quality, light and tough, with light-brown heartwood and yellowish-white sapwood. It lasts almost indefinitely even without preservative treatment. This is the cedar that is used so extensively, in Britain as well as in America, for roofing shingles, sheds, greenhouses, and bungalows. Small poles are excellent for ladders. The green winter foliage is used for Christmas decorations.

Young seedlings of western red cedar are often seriously attacked at the nursery stage by the Keithia disease fungus, and many plants are killed. Thus it is difficult to raise seedlings successfully, except in remote nurseries that have not yet become infected by the disease. As older tissues are not attacked, it is possible, though expensive, to raise young trees from cuttings.

21. White Cedar, *Thuja occidentalis*

(For 'cedar', see No. 20.) This species is called 'white' because of the pale under-surface of its foliage. The name *Thuja* comes from an ancient Greek name for a North African conifer with scented wood.

White cedar has flatter shoots than western red cedar. The lower-side of the shoots is definitely paler than the green upper-side. The leaves

have distinctly arched and rounded glands. The branching is less regular than in the last species, and the cones are slightly smaller.

White cedar is an extremely variable species, with many different forms in colour and habit. It is native to eastern North America and was one of the first American trees to be introduced (in 1596) into Europe; it grows up to 64 ft. tall.

In this country it is of no value for normal forest planting on account of its slow growth. However, this tree is very hardy in our northern climate and is used to a considerable extent in its many garden varieties as an ornamental tree or for hedges.

22. Lawson Cypress, *Chamaecyparis lawsoniana*

Both the English name and the Latin specific name were given in honour of the Scottish nurseryman Peter Lawson of Edinburgh, who engaged the botanist William Murray to explore North America for rare trees. 'Cypress' is basically connected with the Latin *cupressus*, applied to a European cypress to which Lawson cypress is related.

Like all species of *Chamaecyparis*, Lawson cypress has round cones with shield-shaped woody cone scales. In contrast to western red cedar, which it closely resembles, it has a pendulous leading shoot. The shoots are narrower and finer; the upper-sides are green, and the undersides have irregular white to whitish-grey markings.

Lawson cypress comes from southern Oregon and was introduced to Europe in 1854. At first this tree was confined to gardens and parks and very many varieties of form and colour were planted; some grow up to 102 ft. tall. Later it came to be used as a forest tree. The foliage is much in demand for decorations.

The wood is light, with brownish heartwood and light sapwood, and contains scented, ethereal oils which are repellent to moths, etc. Cupboards and chests made of Lawson cypress wood are moth-proof. It is used for general joinery, box-making, and furniture.

23. Juniper, *Juniperus communis*

'Juniper' is taken from the tree's Latin name of *juniperus*. The Gaelic name is *aiteann*, a word linked with *teine* meaning fire, because of the use of its twigs for kindling. In Ireland it is called *iubhar creige*, yew of the rocks, and in Wales *meryw*, dwarf yew.

The various species of juniper form a special group within the cypress family. They are characterized by their berry-like cones, the scales of which are not separate and woody like those of other conifers, but are grown together, and are rather juicy and fleshy.

The common juniper, which grows wild in Britain, is characterized by its awl-shaped, tapering needles, which are borne in whorls of three. The upper-side of the

needle is bluish-green, while the under-side is dark green.

Common juniper is normally dioecious, that is the male and female flowers are only to be found on separate trees, although there are occasional individuals that bear flowers of both sexes. Both male and female flowers appear before the shoots lengthen in May and June. The male flowers are yellow and easy to see, while the female flowers are greenish and somewhat inconspicuous. The berry-like cones, which take two years to ripen, are green or bluish-green in the first year, and in the second year are dark blue and covered with a white waxy coating.

The bark is thin, greyish-brown to reddish-brown, but with age it becomes frayed and peels off in small flakes. Juniper wood is durable and tough; it has reddish-brown heartwood and yellowish-white sapwood. The smell of the wood is characteristic and somewhat resembles that of good quality pencils, which are in fact made of an American species of juniper.

The larger sizes of juniper wood can be used for high quality woodwork. The thinner and curved branches are used for basket-work, and the small twigs are used for smoking and curing foodstuffs.

As a rule, juniper is a thickly

Distribution of juniper
(including dwarf juniper)

branched bush, but the form varies considerably from a flat, creeping or prostrate plant about 2 ft. high, to a single stemmed tree of up to 35 ft.

The cones or 'berries', which contain about 1 per cent oil of juniper, have some medicinal and antiseptic properties. Today, however, the principal use of juniper berries is for flavouring gin.

A small aphid causes the characteristic needle-galls, or 'whooping berries', which were said to be a remedy for whooping cough.

Common juniper is native in Europe, North Africa, northern Asia and North America and thus has the greatest range of all conifers. In Britain it is common both amid the Highland pinewoods of Scotland and on the chalk downs of the south. The dwarf juniper, *Juniperus nana*, found in the north of Scotland, has small soft needles adpressed to the stem, with broad white bands on their inner sides; it grows about 2 ft. high.

Willow Family, Salicaceae.

24. Aspen, *Populus tremula*
(also called **Aspen poplar**)

'Poplar' is a borrowed name which has come from the Latin *populus*. The Welsh form is *poplys*. *Populus* is connected with the Greek *paipallo* meaning tremors (cf. French *papillon*, butterfly). It must refer to the 'trembling' leaves of the aspen, which certainly live up to this description. The meaning of the word 'aspen' is unknown, but it occurs as *aesp* in Anglo-Saxon.

In Gaelic this tree is called *eubh* and in Welsh *aethnen*. Two other names record the incessant motion of its leaves—the Gaelic *cran critheach*, quivering tree, and the Welsh *coed tafod merched*, tree of the woman's tongue.

Aspen has leaves and buds typical of its group of poplars. The leaves

are nearly round, with indented edges; the leaf-stalks are very long and flattened, and the buds glabrous, pointed, and not sticky.

Like all poplars, aspen is dioecious (with separate male and female individuals) and the flowers are contained in long pendulous catkins. The male catkins are a handsome light red. The fruit capsules contain many quite small seeds, and these are covered with cottony down which helps them to be dispersed by the wind. The seed germinates immediately and will not tolerate storage. Aspen flowers in March to April, and comes into leaf in early May. The leaves have beautiful autumn colouring, varying from golden yellow to red and purple.

The bark of young trees is smooth and whitish-grey to yellowish-grey, but later it becomes dark grey and rugged.

The root system has many shallow adventitious roots, from which numerous suckers often develop. The leaves of these suckers differ considerably from the leaves in the crown of the tree, as they are ovate-cordate, pointed, short-stalked and

often very large. Aspen varies widely in the form and size of leaves, date of flushing and in the tree form (weeping, pyramidal).

Aspen is one of the oldest known trees in northern Europe, and evidence of it has been found in bogs in layers from the first Dryas period (see p. 206 et seq.). It is a light-demanding tree which will not stand competition from trees casting shade.

However, in Britain the aspen is normally a tree of little value, especially in the smaller woodlands and on poor heathlands, where it is usually small-leaved and bushy.

Aspen extends over the greater part of Europe, to North Africa, and through Asia to Japan.

As in all the aspen group, but in contrast to some other poplars, the timber has no distinct heartwood. It is white, light, porous and easy to cleave. On account of these characteristics its chief use is in the manufacture of matches, but it is also extremely suitable for the production of high quality paper, and is also used for the interior parts of furniture.

In forest genetics much work is being done with the hybrids between European aspen and the American form, *Populus tremuloides*. These cross-strains are decidedly faster growing, and are almost resistant to poplar rust.

25. White Polar, *Populus alba*

The name 'white poplar' refers to the down, which is snow-white on young shoots and the lower-surfaces of young leaves; on the older leaves of the short shoots, the down is more silver-white and remains so throughout the summer. In the eastern counties, white poplar, together with grey poplar, is sometimes called 'abele'. This word has come via the Low German *Abeel*, from the French *aubel* which is derived from the Latin *albellus*, white.

The white poplar group may be recognized by the leaves of the young, fast-growing shoots, which, like the buds, are white or grey felted; also by the leaf stalk, which is almost round, not flattened as in other poplars.

In the common white poplar, which is a representative of this group, the leaves of the suckers and

long shoots are palmately veined and palmately lobed, and the under-surfaces are bright silver-white. The leaves of the short shoots are ovate-cordate, with indented edges, and are often nearly glabrous.

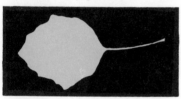

White poplar, which can be a large tree up to 95 ft., is indigenous to Europe and Asia, including Britain, and is often planted as an ornamental tree. Sometimes it is used for a hedge or windbreak; it is valuable for this purpose near the coast, for it stands up to salt winds. It produces many suckers—a disadvantage in a garden, but useful where dense low shelter is needed.

26. Grey Poplar, *Populus canescens*

The name 'grey poplar' refers to the down covering on the under-sides of the leaves, which is not snow-white as in the white poplar. The down wears off in the course of two months, so that the crown appears greyish-green in the middle of the summer.

This poplar also belongs to the white poplar group, but is distinguished from the true white poplar by the leaves of the suckers and the long shoots, which are never palmately lobed, and by the leaves of the short shoots which are usually somewhat larger, more rounded, and sometimes very glabrous.

Grey poplar is considered by some authorities to be a hybrid between aspen and white poplar, while others regard it as a separate species in its own right.

Grey poplar is native in Britain—it has approximately the same geographical range as white poplar. On account of its great resistance to wind, it is often used in windbreaks. The more regular form of the suckers and the extensive and superficial root system make it suitable for planting to give shelter along field boundaries and elsewhere, especially near the sea.

The rapid growth and graceful form of the grey poplar make it especially suitable for an ornamental tree, and it may become up to 110 ft. high, and 17 ft. round.

27. Berlin Poplar,
Populus berolinensis

Berlin poplar originated in Berlin.

This tree is a hybrid between the Lombardy poplar and the Asiatic balsam poplar, *Populus laurifolia*. It is not so columnar as Lombardy poplar, but has a small crown and erect branches. It has inherited from black poplar a very narrow translucent leaf margin, and from balsam poplar the round leaf stalk. The buds are sticky, and the young shoots downy and somewhat angled. The almost ovate and pointed leaves have stomata on the upper surface.

Berlin poplar thrives on soil of moderate fertility, and is fast growing; it is therefore used in windbreaks. Recent years have shown that in some localities it is liable to the various poplar diseases and it has not fulfilled its early promise.

28. Lombardy Poplar,
Populus nigra italica

Lombardy poplar is a 'sport' or freak variety of the wild black poplar. It has a narrow plume-like form, and does not develop the broad crown of the type. It is called 'Lombardy' poplar because the tree is commonly grown on the plains of Northern Italy.

The black poplar group, to which the Lombardy poplar belongs, have leaves with narrow but clearly translucent margins. In addition, on their upper-surfaces the leaves have stomata which when seen through a lens look like small grey spots. The leaf stalk is very compressed, and the buds are rather sticky and scented.

While the typical black poplar, *Populus nigra*, is very seldom planted, Lombardy poplar, the columnar variety, is frequently used in parks, gardens and windbreaks, or as screens to hide ugly buildings. It may be recognized by the characteristic diamond-shaped and pointed leaves, which are light green in spring. They are serrated above the middle, and have many glands at the leaf base. The young shoots are glabrous and round.

Black poplar and its varieties range from Portugal to the Caspian sea, and from Cyprus to England.

Nearly all the Lombardy poplars in Britain are male, as they have all been obtained by vegetative propagation of one individual tree (vegetative propagation consists of cuttings, grafting, layering, etc.). Male trees are preferred because they do not shed the downy seeds that make gardens look untidy.

The timber of the typical black poplar is useful for matches, joinery and paper pulp. But that of the Lombardy poplar is so irregular and full of knots that it is useless.

The many species of poplar are often difficult to identify. One feature often present is a small aphid called *Pemphigus spirothecae*. This insect causes characteristic galls on the leaf stalks of poplar, but they are only found on black poplar, its varieties, and some of the hybrids, and not, for example, on Canadian poplar.

The typical black poplar can become a very big tree, up to 140 ft. tall and 27 ft. round; Lombardy poplar grows up to 108 ft. high.

29. Black Italian Poplar,
Populus serotina

This particular form of black poplar is called 'Italian' from the mistaken belief that it arose in Italy.

Black Italian poplar is a late-leafing hybrid between two black poplars, the American *Populus deltoides* and the European *Populus nigra*. The cross has been made several times, but most of the black Italian poplars one sees have been increased vegetatively (in this case by cuttings) from a very few original hybrids.

Such a collection of trees, raised vegetatively from one 'mother' tree, is called a clone, and a feature of a clone is that each individual has the same inherited potentiality as the parent tree. Therefore individual trees in a clone, if grown under the same conditions, look, and indeed are, very much alike. Nearly all our black Italian poplars are males, although female trees are known.

The leaf of black Italian poplar is pointed, serrated, and triangular-

ovate, with a cordate or slightly truncate base. At the side of the stalk on the leaf base there are usually one or two glands. These are bronze coloured in the spring. The young shoots are smooth, especially the most angular ones.

Flowering takes place in April to May. The conspicuous red male catkins soon fall off.

Black Italian poplar is one of the oldest of the many poplar hybrids which are known. It arose in France in about 1750, and perhaps in other places; on account of its rapid growth and good stem form it has frequently been planted. In some places, along roadsides and field boundaries, it has quickly become a tree of massive proportions and has been pollarded, so that the branches can be obtained more easily for hurdle-making, etc.

30. Ontario Poplar,
Populus candicans (P. gileadensis)

The name refers to the province in Canada where this species was found.

This tree belongs to the balsam poplar group. The characteristic features are very large, sticky and strongly scented buds; the margin of the leaf is irregular and the leaf stalk is rounded; the under-surfaces of the leaves of all these species are white to greyish-white.

Ontario poplar has large heart-shaped leaves, the lower-surfaces of which are white, and a distinctly hairy leaf stalk. The young branches are round and hairy. The buds are large and very sticky, being covered with scented resin. This species grows into a very large tree, up to 105 ft., often with a rather crooked stem. The bark of old stems is furrowed.

The tree is hardy and windfirm and is sometimes used as an ornamental tree and for hedges or windbreaks. But although it is vigorous, it has the disadvantage of producing thickets of sucker shoots, and its planting should be avoided.

Flowering takes place from April to May. The female catkins are large, and the seed is covered with much cottony down.

31. Oregon Balsam Poplar,
Populus trichocarpa

The name of this species refers first to its American homeland and then to its scented resin, which contains ethereal oils and is called 'balsam'.

Oregon balsam poplar grows into a large tree, and the bark becomes furrowed at an early age. The young shoots are rather angled and slightly hairy, and the leaves are ovate to ob-

long diamond-shaped, with yellowish-white net-veined under-sides. The buds are long and strongly scented.

This species grows along the Pacific coast of North America from Alaska to California.

This tree is described here although it is not yet a particularly important one, as there are reasons for believing that it will gain ground for windbreaks and also for timber production. It grows vigorously in the high-rainfall regions of western Britain, and reaches heights around 90 ft. Some strains of it are resistant to canker.

32. Goat Willow, Sallow, *Salix caprea*

The willows are remarkable in having a range of English names derived from several roots, thus:

'Willow', from Anglo-Saxon *welig*, pliant.

'Withy', from Anglo-Saxon *withig* and Norse *vithir*, allied to Latin *vitis*, a vine.

'Sallow', from Anglo-Saxon *sealh*, allied to Latin *salix*, French *saule*, Gaelic *seileach*, Welsh *helyg* and Danish *selje*.

'Saugh', commonly used in Scotland, from Gaelic *seileach*.

'Osier', from French *osiere*, Latin *ausaria*, a willow bed.

In the north of England willows are called 'palm' trees, because their catkins are used for Easter decorations. 'Goat' willow, like the Latin *Salix caprea*, indicates that the leaves are a favourite food of domestic goats, especially in spring.

While the buds of other trees and bushes consist of several bud scales, or are occasionally without scales, the willows have *one* single hood-shaped and double-keeled bud scale.

The separate sorts of willow are very difficult to identify without special knowledge, and we have therefore described here only the most common wild and planted species.

The willows are divided into 'spring willows' and 'summer willows'. 'Spring willows', which are mostly bushes or small trees, bear flowers before the leaves have appeared. The unstalked catkins grow on short uniform dwarf shoots, which seldom have leaves and then only very few small ones. 'Spring willows' include goat willow, eared willow, grey willow, creeping willow, Caspian willow and common osier.

'Summer willows' are mostly small bushes and trees. They bloom later; at the time of, or after, coming into leaf they produce stalked catkins on leaf-bearing side shoots. Bay-leaved willow, crack and white willow belong to this class. Like poplars, willows are dioecious.

Goat willow is one of the few British willows which is included in the forest community as a small tree, up to 30 ft. in height. It is often found outside the forest, usually as a bush about 10 ft. high.

It is recognized by its very large elliptical to rounded leaves, with dark green, smooth upper-surfaces and greyish-white felted under-surfaces. The young branches are downy in the first year, but afterwards become smooth and turn a greyish-brown colour. The buds—especially the flower buds—are large and have a characteristic thick and recurved apex.

The catkins come out very early (often in March) and are among the first flowers of importance to bee-keepers, as willow pollen and honey make an excellent food for bees. It may also be mentioned here that very few of our forest trees are pollinated by insects. Nearly all are wind-pollinated, and quantities of free pollen are spread by the wind and caught by the viscid stigmas. This sometimes happens with willow pollen also.

The yellow pollen, at the time of flowering, makes the male catkins of goat willow and other willows very conspicuous. The female catkins, with their greenish-yellow stigmas, are less conspicuous. The fruit, as in all willows, is a double-lobed capsule, and the seeds, which cannot easily be stored, are covered with cottony down. The bark is greyish-green and remains smooth for a long time before becoming furrowed and rugged. It contains about 10 per cent tannin and can be used for tanning leather. In addition, the bark contains salicin, from which salicylic acid, a medicinal drug, may be obtained.

The wood of goat willow is soft and the sapwood is whitish-yellow. The heartwood is an inconspicuous light reddish-yellow. There is no particular use for this wood, but gypsies harvest it for clothes-pegs.

Goat willow grows wild in most of Europe and Asia.

33. Eared Willow, *Salix aurita*

The name of 'eared' willow refers to the stipules, which are shaped like ears and appear in twos at the base of some of the leaves, but only on the more vigorous shoots. Ear-shaped stipules occur also in some other species of willow.

Eared willow is a small bush about 6 ft. high, with fine, often reddish, smooth branches and buds. The leaves are small obovate, with grey hairs on both sides, and somewhat twisted tips. The under-surfaces of the leaves are veined, and the stipules are kidney-shaped.

This species is usually found on damp acid ground, for example in heathland scrub on the edge of bogs.

34. Grey Willow, *Salix cinerea*

Called 'grey' willow from the greyish appearance of its downy branches and buds.

Grey willow is larger and coarser than eared willow, which it resembles in appearance, but the branches are hairy and the buds downy, and the leaves are larger and often lance-shaped, with a twisted tip.

Grey willow is usually found on the wetter sites, but it is not confined to acid soils. It grows up to 10 ft. high.

35. Creeping Willow, *Salix repens*

The name refers to the habit of growth.

Creeping willow is a dwarf bush seldom more than 3 ft. high; often it does not grow above the surrounding vegetation. The silver-coloured leaves are small, oval to oblong and, underneath at least, covered with silky hairs.

Creeping willow is common in bogs, heaths, sand dunes and plantations on sandy soils. It is very variable and can be divided into three groups or types, of which the first has just been described. The second is the sub-species *arenaria*, which has wider to almost rounded

silky-haired leaves and, unlike the other forms, distinct stipules. This form is only found in sand dune areas. It will grow in drifting sand and produce roots many yards long and thus has a very effective sand fixation effect. For this reason its gathering was prohibited on the Danish sand dunes as early as 1475.

The third sub-species of creeping willow is *rosmarinifolia*. This has narrow, oblong and less hairy leaves,

and in comparison with the former types it becomes a tall bush with fine branches.

It is found on boggy ground rich in nutrients, but is very uncommon.

36. Caspian Willow,
Salix acutifolia

So named after its homeland; it grows wild in Russia and Siberia.

Caspian willow is occasionally planted in place of the violet willow (No. 36a) which it closely resembles, but the blue-spotted branches are dark reddish-violet and the leaf

stalk is glabrous. It flowers slightly sooner in March, and as early as December the silver-covered catkins can be seen.

Both these willows have been used as wands for basketry.

36a. Violet Willow,
Salix daphnoides

So called from the attractive violet-brown colour of its winter twigs.

Violet willow is a hardy and tolerant tree which, unlike most other willows, grows best on ground that is not too damp. It has narrow lanceolate and pointed leaves, with downy-haired leaf stalks. The young shoots are greenish-brown, and in winter and in time of drought they are blue-spotted.

Violet willow is one of the earliest and most used of the decorative willows; the trees produce silver-white catkins early in winter, and are often in full flower in March.

It is not native in Britain, but its area of distribution is eastern Europe, and western and central Asia.

37. Common Osier,
Salix viminalis

For the name origin see No. 32.

Common osier has very long (up to 10 in.) linear-lanceolate leaves, with revolute margins and white undersides. Branches and buds are hairy.

Osier grows into a bush or small tree and is planted along fences and hedgerows; but it is principally grown because the young shoots, which are produced annually after each cutting, are most suitable for basket-work.

This species grows wild in the eastern counties, and is widely distributed in Europe and Asia.

38. Crack Willow, *Salix fragilis*

The name refers to the tree's brittle-ness. This brittleness, which is apparent when the tree has reached a certain age, is especially evident in the angles of the twigs and branches, and is also found to some degree in the timber.

With crack willow we come to the 'summer willows', which are characterized by their late date of flowering. Crack willow usually becomes a large tree up to 50 ft. high, which can be distinguished at a distance by its open crown and almost right-angled, wide-spreading branches. These are easily broken off by the wind, and branches may, under favourable conditions, take root.

The leaves are wide, lance-shaped, acuminate and glabrous. On the dull light-green upper-surfaces small grey spots resembling stomata are visible under a lens. The under-surfaces are pale grey.

Crack willow is a common wild tree, especially along river-sides in the Midlands.

39. White Willow, *Salix alba*

The name 'white willow' refers to the greyish-white colour that the leaves of many white willows have, owing to their silky hairs.

White willow is a large and beautiful tree, up to 81 ft. high; however, it is often pollarded. The young shoots and the lower-surfaces of the lance-shaped leaves, and some-times also the upper-surfaces, are covered with rather dense silky hairs. As in crack willow there are stomata on the upper-surfaces of the leaves. The twigs are not brittle, except perhaps at the base.

There are many varieties of white willow, of which those with pendu-lous branches are most frequently planted (weeping willow, hanging willow). Another form often seen is characterized in winter by shoots which are red, like storks' legs. A rather special variety, probably a hybrid between white willow and crack willow, is cricket bat willow (*Salix alba* var. *coerulea*). It makes very rapid growth on ground which is damp and preferably occasionally flooded, but also rich in nutrients, and the wood is particularly suitable for the manufacture of cricket bats.

White willow and its varieties are frequently planted along roadsides and fences, and in parks and gardens. Some types provide material for basket-work.

White willow is native in central Europe, North Africa and Asia, as well as in Britain.

40. Bay-Leaved Willow, *Salix pentandra*

So called from the resemblance of its leaves to those of the sweet bay tree, *Laurus nobilis*.

Bay-leaved willow is a large bush or small tree (up to 40 ft. high) with smooth shiny branches which grad-ually become dark brown.

The shiny, fresh-green leaves are narrowly ovate, pointed, and finely serrated. They somewhat resemble the leaves of crack willow, but differ in that the upper surfaces are not covered with stomata.

Flowering is very late and takes place when the plant comes into leaf in May. The male catkins, which are a beautiful golden yellow, normally contain five stamens, but there may be more. Both the flowers and the leaves have an aromatic scent.

The seed capsules open very late, and the seeds are dispersed in the winter. Female trees may be recognized at a distance when the seeds are being dispersed, as each one of the many catkins looks like a piece of cotton wool, owing to the masses of woolly down on the opening capsules.

Bay willow is found especially in fens which are rich in nutrients, and on the edge of lakes; it is common throughout Britain. It grows up to latitude 70° N. and extends over most of Europe and Siberia.

Myrica Family, Myricaceae.

41. Sweet Gale, Bog Myrtle,
Myrica gale

The name 'gale' comes from Anglo-Saxon *gayel*, but its meaning is uncertain; 'sweet' refers to the aromatic odour. 'Myrtle' derives, via French *myrtille*, from the Latin *myrtus* for the true myrtle tree, while 'bog' refers to the usual habitat.

Sweet gale is a thickly branched bush about 3 ft. high. The leaves are alternate, dark green, serrated only at the apex, and wedge-shaped at the base. The young shoots are reddish-brown, downy and, like the leaves, are covered with small aromatic resin glands.

Flowering generally takes place in March to April, before the leaves have come out. Male plants are easily recognizable by the large male catkin buds which remain through the winter. On female plants the catkin buds appear about one month before flowering. The male catkins are about ½ in. long, with reddish-brown scales. Female catkins are shorter (¼ in.) and less conspicuous. Each female flower has two long red stamens. The fruit, which is a drupe, is covered with yellow glands.

Sweet gale propagates itself by producing many suckers and can, in this way, cover a very large area. The roots have a number of nodules which contain the mycelium of a fungus, with the help of which sweet gale is able to utilize the nitrogen in the air. This plant grows best on damp acid soils, and is therefore frequently found near heathland ponds, and bogs on low ground. Its geographical distribution is very extensive and, over the greater part of this range, it is a plant of the coastal regions. Sweet gale grows wild in western, central and northern Europe and northern North America.

In former times sweet gale was used instead of hops in the brewing of beer, and the shoots with their aromatic scent have been used as a protection against mosquitoes and other insect pests. An extract containing alcohol can be obtained from the fruits, which are covered with glands, and from the young twigs.

Birch Family, Betulaceae.

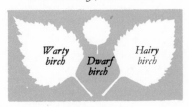

Warty birch   Dwarf birch   Hairy birch

42. Warty Birch,
Betula pendula (*B. verrucosa*)

'Birch' is the English form of 'birk', still used in Scotland. This name 'birk' is one of the most common Teutonic tree names. It is of Indo-Germanic origin.

Other names are: Danish, *birk*; Swedish, *bjork*; German, *Birke*; French, *bouleau*; Welsh, *bedw*; and

Gaelic *beith*. This particular species is also called 'silver' birch, but as that name is often loosely applied, it is better to use the name 'warty' birch, which indicates a distinctive feature of the twigs.

The birch species which we shall describe have, among other characteristics, the following features. The development of the shoot is sympodial: that is, the terminal bud dies away and is replaced by a side bud. Shoots are divided into short shoots and long shoots. The male catkins, which grow at the end of the long shoots, appear in the autumn before they flower, and remain ripe during the winter; the female catkins, which grow on the leaf-bearing short shoots, first appear when the tree comes into leaf. Another characteristic of birch is that the catkin scales fall off at the same time as the winged nuts, when the latter are ripe.

Warty birch grows into a tree up to 102 ft. tall. It has at first a bright golden-brown bark, which with age becomes white as the bark cambium produces papery tissues containing betulin, which reflects the light. The bark remains smooth for a long time, and peels off in thin flakes. Old trees have very irregular, dark and rugged bark.

The young branches are more or less covered with greyish-white resin warts, but otherwise the branches are smooth and shiny. The shoots are slender and the youngest ones are often very thin and pendulous (hence the name weeping or hanging birch). The buds are small and sticky.

The leaves unfold in late April and are at first sticky with resin; this dries when the leaves are older, leaving white scales. The base of the fully-developed leaf is entire, slightly truncate, or broadly wedge-shaped. The leaves are acuminate and doubly serrated. They turn yellow early and fall in October.

The flowers appear a short time after the leaves; the fruits ripen in July. The seeds are spread by the wind and are so numerous that they often cover the ground in and around birch stands. The wings of the fruit of warty birch are longer and wider than the actual seeds, and the side lobes of the catkin scales curve downwards.

The wood is whitish, and sometimes has small brown spots (pith flecks) due to insect attack; there is no distinct heartwood. The wood has many uses including furniture, veneers, plywoods, skis, parquet blocks, turnery and broom heads.

In some specimens of warty birch the fibres of the wood are very irregular and form a structure with a distinctive appearance. This curly-grained wood is very valuable.

Birch is a valuable firewood and the logs make an attractive fire. The twigs have been much used for making brooms and are also used in buoys, for marking out sailing channels. Birch bark has had many different uses, including roofing shingles and shoes.

If birch trees are cut in the spring, a great deal of sap flows from the wounds. This sap contains sugar

and can be fermented to make wine.

Warty birch and its varieties extend over the whole of the British Isles. It is a light-demander and grows best on dry ground. With aspen it is a pioneer tree on areas devastated by forest fires.

Warty birch grows throughout the greater part of Europe and the Caucasus.

43. Hairy Birch, *Betula pubescens*

Although this species is also called 'white' birch, that name leads to confusion with the previous species. 'Hairy' birch, referring to the distinctive hairy shoots, is better.

Hairy birch may be distinguished from warty birch by its stiffer branching habit. In addition, the buds are usually slightly longer and stickier. The leaves are more wedge-shaped at the base, and the blade is not so pointed and is only slightly serrated.

The young branches have velvety hairs and are without resin warts. The tiny seeds or nuts are larger than those of the warty birch, while the wings are of about the same length and breadth as the seeds. The side lobes of the catkin scales are shorter, and curve upwards.

On old trees the bark is not so uneven and cracked as that of warty birch, and it tends to peel off in horizontal strips.

Hairy birch grows mainly on wet or moist sites, round lakes and in bogs. It is the first species to gain a footing on swampy ground that will support any kind of tree growth. It grows about 70 ft. tall.

Hairy birch is found all over the British Isles, and its total range extends from Greenland and Iceland over northern and central Europe, through Siberia to Kamtschatka.

44. Dwarf Birch, *Betula nana*

Dwarf birch is a small bush up to about 3 ft. high. It is thickly branched and the young shoots are vertical. The leaves are small, rounded and regularly serrated. The upper-surfaces are dark green, and the lower-surfaces lighter green and clearly ribbed. The male and female catkins are erect. The winged seeds or nuts are broadly ovate with short narrow wings. The female catkin scale is divided into three narrow and upright lobes.

The home of dwarf birch is in mountain and highland moors and bogs, especially in the Arctic. It was one of the first of the tree species to spread into Northern Europe after the Ice Age, and is still found in the far north of Scotland. Apart from Arctic regions of Europe, Asia and America, it is found as a relic of colder ages in high-lying districts of southern Sweden, and in a few high bogs in northern Germany.

45. Common Alder,
Alnus glutinosa

The name 'alder' comes from Anglo-Saxon *aler* and Norse *eller*, and is related to German *Erle*. The Gaelic name is *fearn* and the Welsh *gwern;* these, like 'alder' and 'eller', are common elements in place names.

Common alder — Grey alder

In both common alder and grey alder the shoots have a well-developed terminal bud (monopodial branching) and the buds are stalked. The male and female catkins develop in the autumn and remain bare during the winter. While the female catkins are ripening, they become woody and resemble small cones. Another feature of both species is that the roots develop

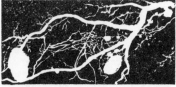

nodules which contain the mycelia of a fungus. With the help of this fungus the roots are able to utilize the free nitrogen of the air.

When growing under favourable conditions, common alder may reach a height of up to 70 ft. When young the stem has a continuous axis, but when older it develops the typical arched crown composed of crooked branches.

The young branches are smooth, covered with resin warts, and rather sticky. The bark on young trees is smooth, shiny and greenish-brown. Older trees have a dark grey rugged bark. The stalked buds are brownish-violet and rather sticky. The leaves, which unfold at the beginning of May, are alternate, singly serrated and oval. The upper-surfaces are dark green, and at first slightly sticky; the lower-surfaces are lighter green, with rust-brown hairs in the angles of the veins. Common alder is one of the few

trees with leaves which remain green in the autumn, almost until they fall.

Flowering takes place very early, from March to the beginning of April. The male catkins are long and pendulous; the female catkins are small and upright or projecting. The female catkins, after over-wintering, become thick and green during the summer and, after the fruit has ripened in October, the catkin scales begin to get woody. Most of the seeds are dispersed in the following spring.

In spring, three generations of female catkins can be seen on both common alder and grey alder: the black woody catkins, whose seed has fallen and has been dispersed by the wind; the green immature catkins; and the small female catkins, which will remain on the tree during the winter. In common alder each female catkin is clearly stalked; this is one of the obvious features that distinguish it from grey alder, as female catkins of the latter are not stalked.

The seeds, like those of grey alder, are small, flat, reddish-brown nuts. They are edged with air-filled webbing which enables them to remain floating on water for about a month. The seeds may be carried considerable distances in streams and on oars, and are widely distributed in this way.

Common alder grows best on damp ground rich in nutrients; for example, near streams and lakes, and on swampy ground, where it often forms small woods. In swamps common alder has a characteristic appearance, as if it were standing on 'stilts'. These stilts are in fact supporting roots growing out from the stem into the soil. They are often seen on the stool shoots which common alder frequently produces from the stumps of felled trees, and in the course of time the original stumps rot while the vigorous supporting roots remain.

The wood of common alder is whitish-yellow when first felled, but on exposure to air it quickly assumes a brick-red colour, becoming paler as the wood dries. The wood often contains dark brown 'pith flecks', caused by the larvae of an Agromyzid fly.

The wood has many uses, including clogs, turnery, mouldings, window frames, toys, blocks and cheap pencils. It is also used for the imitation of other and more expensive woods, and takes paint and polish well.

The wood of common alder is used in Denmark for burning in smoking and curing processes. The charcoal is used in the manufacture of gunpowder.

Common alder extends over the whole of Europe, from latitude 64° N. to latitude 37° N., and into Siberia, the Caucasus and Asia Minor.

46. Grey Alder, *Alnus incana*

Called 'grey' from the whitish colour of the under-sides of the leaves.

Grey alder may be distinguished from the foregoing species by the hairy annual shoots and buds, smooth light bark, sessile female catkins, and the different leaf form. The leaves are ovate, pointed, deeply serrated, and grey-felted on the lower surfaces.

Grey alder is not so tall as common alder and does not exceed 60 ft. in height. Flowering takes place about three weeks earlier, in mild winters from the end of February, while the leaves break bud later. The fruits are a little larger.

Unlike common alder, grey alder reproduces itself abundantly by suckers. It is more tolerant of soil conditions, but generally prefers ground that is not so wet.

The wood, which does not have a red colour after being felled, is considered to be of a somewhat lower quality.

On woodland planting areas, large plants of grey alder are sometimes widely spaced through the main species of timber-producing tree, to provide protection against sun and frost. It was introduced to British forests with this object in view, but has not proved a success.

But it is a useful tree for planting as a screen on old coal tips and similar waste ground.

In addition to Scandinavia, grey alder is found in central Europe, the north-western parts of European Russia, the Caucasus and the mountains of northern Persia.

Hazel Family, Corylaceae.

47. Hornbeam, *Carpinus betulus*

The word 'beam', closely related to the German *Baum*, is an old Anglo-Saxon word for 'tree'. 'Hornbeam' signifies the tree with the hard or horny-textured wood.

Hornbeam grows to a height of about 75 ft. The arched crown and smooth light-grey bark of this tree are reminiscent of beech. In most other trees a cross-section of the stem is regular and almost circular, but a section of hornbeam has an irregular shape which shows that even in youth the stem was longitudinally fluted.

The terminal buds on the shoots die away and are replaced by the

first side buds, and the branching is therefore sympodial. The bud scales are placed in four rows; the leaf buds are slender and pointed, and pressed closely against the twigs. The buds which produce the catkins containing the male flowers are larger than the leaf buds, and not adpressed. In the spring the buds are mottled.

The leaves, which are alternate and in two rows, are narrowly ovate, pointed, deeply serrated and very clearly ribbed.

In early May the leaves unfold— a little later than those of beech—

and flowering takes place at the same time. The male flowers come from buds which bear flowers only and not leaves, and are usually on the lowest part of the previous year's shoot. As is usual with wind-pollinated trees, large quantities of pollen are produced by the flowers. The female catkins, with red stigmas, are situated at the end of short annual shoots, and come from buds which also contain leaves. Female flowers are borne in twos in the axils of the long and thin catkin scales (bracts), which soon fall off. The nut is half-enclosed by a three-lobed wing which serves as a sail

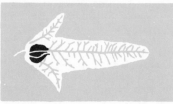

when the fruit is dispersed by the wind. The nuts are $\frac{1}{4}-\frac{1}{2}$ in. long, and are longitudinally ribbed.

As a forest tree, hornbeam has a very limited use, as it grows too slowly for this purpose. On the other hand it is often used for hedges, as it stands cutting very well. Unlike beech it is not damaged by grazing animals.

The wood is yellowish-white, heavy, tough and hard, without apparent heartwood. Wavy annual rings are characteristic. It is an excellent firewood, and in addition has a number of special uses, for tool handles, wooden screws, rollers, lasts and pegs. It was formerly considered to be the most suitable wood for cam-wheels and cog-wheels in mills.

In Britain hornbeam is confined, as a wild tree, to the south-eastern counties. Extensive coppices, once tended for firewood, are found in Kent, Essex, and Hertfordshire. Otherwise it extends over the whole of Europe (with the exception of the Iberian peninsula) and to the Caucasus and Asia Minor.

48. Hazel, *Corylus avellana*

The word 'hazel' is the modern form of the Anglo-Saxon *haesel*, related to Danish *hassel* and German *Hasel*, and possibly derived from the root *hase*, signifying the husk around the nut. The Gaelic name is *caltuinn*, and the Welsh *coll*.

Hazel is always a bush, commonly 10–15 ft. high. It is branched from the ground and has brownish or greyish, smooth, shiny bark with a large number of brown lenticels. The young shoots are thickly covered with glandular hairs and the leaves are alternate, short-stalked, cordate to rounded, and have both glandular and ordinary hairs. The leaves are rather like those of elm, but are much softer, and are even, not oblique, at the base. Hazel comes into leaf in early May, and the leaves fall in November.

The male flowers are contained in catkins on short leafless shoots. They are formed during the summer and remain bare over winter, while the female catkins come from buds which also produce leaves. The time of flowering is in February or March, and depends upon the temperature. The male catkins are more affected by the temperature than the female catkins, and it is not unusual for them to produce pollen in an early warm period before the female flowers have come out.

The small female flowers are concealed in the buds, and only the small red protruding pistils are

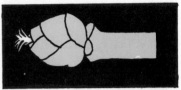

visible. Hazel is often self-sterile (i.e. unable to fertilize itself). In nut plantations different types are therefore planted side by side.

The nuts are enclosed in lobed husks, and there may be up to five clustered together. They ripen in August to September, and somewhat later they fall from the husks. They are thick-shelled and small, but of varying shapes (round and broadly or narrowly oblong). Larger and thinner-shelled types of nuts are produced by selective breeding.

The cotyledons, which are enclosed in the nuts, have a high oil content. They remain under the soil when the seed germinates.

Hazel is often attacked by an almost microscopic gall mite which causes the buds first to swell, and then to fall off.

The wood is white or reddish, soft and easy to cleave, tough and flexible. Hazel rods are used for thatching spars and hurdles, and were formerly employed in wattle-and-daub buildings. Hazel also yields bean rods and pea sticks.

Hazel prefers a soil which is rich

148

in nutrients and not too wet. Early in post-glacial times it formed large stands, mainly under oak and Scots pine. From these came the layer of nuts which may now be found in ancient peat bogs. At the present time it is used as underwood in light oakwoods and in forest boundaries and hedges, and also as a coppice crop, cut at intervals of about seven years, for hurdle rods.

Hazel is common throughout most of Europe, and in North Africa and Asia Minor.

Beech Family, Cupuliferae.

Beech   Pedunculate   Sessile   Red
             oak   oak   oak

49. Beech, *Fagus sylvatica*

The name 'beech' comes from Anglo-Saxon *boece* and old Teutonic *boka*. It is thought to mean edible (fruit), but this is not quite certain. The Welsh name is *ffawydd*, and the Gaelic *feagha*.

Beech is one of the most important broad-leaved trees in the British forests, and may reach a height of

*Forest-grown   Free-standing
beech   beech*

142 ft. In close-canopy forests the stems are clean and free of branches, while free-standing trees are short with very large crowns ('deer park beech'). The bark of the stem is light grey to grey, thin and smooth, and does not normally become rugged with age

The leaves are alternate and placed in two rows, and as the smaller branches are divided into short shoots and long shoots, the leaves form as it were a united surface, called a leaf mosaic. This enables

the tree to utilize the light as effectively as possible, and means that beech is a shade-giving tree, as well as tolerating a certain amount of shade, a condition of importance when competing with other trees. The shade cast by the trees is responsible for the lack of flowers on the forest floor in a beechwood in high summer. However, before the trees are in leaf there may be a considerable flora of early-flowering plants such as anemones, bluebells and primroses.

The buds are projecting, and have scales set in four rows. While the leaf buds are slender and pointed, those buds which contain flowers as well as leaves are definitely thicker

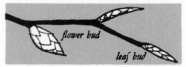

and slightly longer. The difference can be seen a long time before flushing takes place.

Beech begins to come into leaf in late April and early May, and is normally fully in leaf by mid-May. A feature of young trees, clipped hedges, and low branches on old trees, is that some of the leaves remain in the dry and withered state throughout the winter, and fall off shortly before the new leaves come out.

The very young leaves are folded, and are covered with soft, silky hairs; these restrict evaporation and therefore prevent the young tree from dying in periods of drought. In addition the leaves have some protection against night frosts. The fully developed leaves are ovate, entire-margined and somewhat curved on the edges.

Flowering takes place at the same times as the leaves appear. The male catkins contain many flowers, are globular, and hang on a long stalk; the female inflorescences, consisting of two flowers, have short stalks and are enclosed in a prickly husk with four lobes. In each husk, two three-sided nuts are formed. These nuts contain two folded cotyledons which have a high oil content. After germination these cotyledons grow up above the ground; they are kidney-shaped, shiny green above, but whitish below (see illustration, pp. 56–7).

Mast years, that is the years when beech produces abundant fruit, come at varying intervals, depending upon the weather in summer—a warm summer normally causes much flowering next year—and upon the fact that mast years are usually followed by a few years when there is little or no flowering. Again, a late frost, by killing spring blossom, may check a promising mast crop.

In the spring after a mast year the forest soil may be crowded with the characteristic beech seedlings, especially if the soil is harrowed or similarly prepared before the seed falls. These seedlings may, with suitable treatment, be raised to form the next generation of beech.

There are several varieties of beech, including the dark-leaved copper beech, the cut-leaved or fern-leaved beech (illustrated above), and the weeping beech, often planted in parks.

Beech wood is heavy, hard and easily cleft. When first felled it has a whitish-yellow colour, but later becomes light reddish in colour.

The wood has high value as firewood. As timber it has many uses, of which the following may be mentioned: furniture, parquetry blocks, butter casks, tool handles, and small robust wooden articles of all kinds. On the Continent it is used with great success for railway

sleepers. Its natural range includes most of England, south Wales, western Europe to northern Spain, and the greater part of the rest of Europe; the eastern limit runs from East Prussia to the Black Sea. In the southerly regions beech is primarily a mountain tree.

50. Pedunculate Oak,
Quercus robur

'Oak' is the standard form of a word that has many local variants. It is represented by 'aik' in Scotland, 'woke' in the West Country, and 'yak' or 'yuk' in Hampshire. These are derived from the Anglo-Saxon *ac* and the old Teutonic *aiks*.

'Acorn', the seed of the oak, comes from Anglo-Saxon *aecern*, literally oak-corn. The Gaelic name is *darach* and the Welsh *derw*.

This species is distinguished as 'pedunculate' oak since it bears its acorns on long stalks or 'peduncles'.

The pedunculate species is our most common oak. There is a specimen 128 ft. high at Marchmount in East Lothian. The girth may reach considerable dimensions—up to 43 ft. for the Manton Oak in Cheshire.

As a young tree, pedunculate oak has a smooth, shiny and greyish bark, but with age it develops a characteristic rough, furrowed and rugged bark.

The crown of an oak tree is composed of crooked branches and is very open, so that a great deal of light passes through. Thus there is sufficient light for various bushes, as well as many grasses and herbs, to grow in an oakwood—a very different picture from the dark beechwoods.

The leaves begin to appear in late April, but are not fully out until mid-May. The buds are short and plump, with entire margins to the scales. The leaves are very short-stalked, usually glabrous and pinnately lobed. At the leaf base, which

is normally oblique, there are two clearly folded, ear-like lobes (auricles). The lateral veins of the leaf often extend to the tips of the lobes and to the bottoms of the bays. Lammas shoots are very common in oak; these are shoots which appear during summer, so that in one year there are two generations of shoots.

Flowering takes place towards the end of May. The male flowers are enclosed in long hanging catkins, usually on the previous year's shoots, while the flowering female catkins, one to five in number, are upright on fairly long stalks, growing from the upper leaf axils of the annual shoots. The fruits (or acorns) are nuts which are enclosed in a cup at the base. The acorns contain two cotyledons which are bitter and very starchy, but not particularly oily, and which remain in the soil at the time of germination.

The wood of both pedunculate and sessile oak is of excellent quality and is hard and strong. The sapwood is yellowish and comparatively narrow, and is not durable unless treated with preservative. The heartwood is brown to dark brown, and is very durable and resistant to rot. The annual rings and the pith rays are very distinct.

Oak timber throughout the ages has had so many varied uses that many natural oak forests have succumbed to exploitation.

Oak is still used for shipbuilding, especially fishing boats, and for furniture, high quality joinery, parquet flooring, cooperage and fencing.

Oak bark contains a high proportion of tannin and was formerly used in very large quantities in tanneries. In former times acorns were widely used for feeding pigs.

The distribution of pedunculate oak includes the whole of Europe, with the exception of the extreme north and south. In the east it spreads as far as the Caucasus and Asia Minor.

seen under a powerful lens. As a rule the leaves are more regularly shaped, with a larger number of shorter lobes; the lateral veins extend only to the tip of each lobe, and not to the base of each bay. When the leaves wither in the autumn, those on young trees, and on the lower branches of old ones, do not fall, but remain hanging through the winter. The buds are slender and pointed. Sessile oak grows up to 105 ft. tall, and 24 ft. in girth.

Flowering takes place a few days later than in pedunculate oak, and the female flowers, and therefore the fruits, are practically stalkless. The acorns are often somewhat smaller, and more pointed.

In general there is a great likeness between these two species of oak, and as there are intermediate forms, a definite identification is often difficult.

51. Sessile Oak, *Quercus petraea*

Called 'sessile' oak because the acorns are stalkless or nearly so, and sit directly on the twigs.

Sessile oak differs from pedunculate oak in having a straighter growth habit, usually with a continuous axis and more regular branches. The leaves have a distinct stalk $\frac{1}{2}$ to 1 in. long, and the leaf-base is wedge-shaped and does not have 'ears'. The leaves are smooth and more leathery, and their lower surfaces usually have scattered star-shaped (stellate) hairs, which can only be

Sessile oak is found on lighter, more porous soils than common oak, and it often occurs in moun-

tainous regions. Its range is somewhat smaller than that of pedunculate oak. It is the commoner species in the Highlands of Scotland and in the uplands of Wales and northern England.

52. Red Oak, *Quercus borealis*

The name 'red oak' is derived from the autumn colour of the leaves, although older trees turn almost a golden-brown colour.

This oak may reach a height of 102 ft. Isolated trees have a somewhat open crown composed of slightly thicker and straighter branches than those of the two oaks previously described. The young branches quickly become a dark red colour.

The leaves are large, 4–8 in. long, with wedge-shaped leaf bases, and

from seven to eleven pointed, distantly toothed lobes. The upper surfaces are dull green and the lower surfaces bluish-green. Young plants and stool shoots have magnificently red autumn colours.

The acorns of red oak take two years to develop. The first year after pollination they reach the size of small peas, and they achieve full development only in the second year. These acorns are definitely thicker than those of pedunculate and sessile oak, and where attached to the cup are flat or concave. The cup is low, and flattened at the base.

The wood is very porous and is not so valuable as that of the other two oaks. It is used to some extent in the manufacture of furniture.

As a forest tree red oak is used for planting on the more gravelly and sandy soils, where it grows well. As it is also windfirm, it is often used in exposed places. The red autumn leaves are a scenic asset.

Red oak does not grow wild in Europe, but has been introduced from eastern North America.

52a. Sweet Chestnut,
Castanea sativa

The name 'chestnut' comes via old French *chastaigne* from the Latin *castanea*, with the English 'nut'.

This tree (not illustrated) was probably introduced from Italy by the Romans. It is now grown in the south of England as a coppice crop for the production of small poles used in hop fields and for cleft-pale fencing. It can also form a tall tree with a strong and durable heartwood, surrounded by a remarkably narrow, pale sapwood. The leaf of the sweet chestnut resembles that of red oak (No. 52), but with smaller, more regular indentations, and a general outline like the blade of a spear. It is mid-green in colour, turning bright brown when it withers. The fruit resembles that of horse chestnut (No. 98), but the spines on the husk are more numerous and softer, while the nut is more oval and is both sweet and nutritious. The flowering pattern resembles that of the oaks; green male catkins are borne along long stalks in July; the much smaller green female catkins, which arise farther back on the flowering stalks, ripen rapidly to nuts that fall in November. These nuts mature only in our southern counties, where they sometimes give rise to natural seedlings. Nearly all our eating chestnuts are imported from Italy.

Elm Family, Ulmaceae.

53. Wych Elm, Ulmus glabra

The derivation and meaning of the name 'elm' are obscure; it is familiar within the European range of the species, as shown for example in the Swedish alm and the Latin ulmus, which come from the same root as 'elm'. 'Wych' stems from old Teutonic wik, meaning 'to bend', suggesting flexible twigs. The Gaelic name for elm is leamban, and the Welsh llwyfan.

The elms are large trees with rough bark and thick dark green crowns; the branching system is sympodial, and often the branches clearly form two rows.

The flowers come from buds which do not contain leaves, and they are hermaphrodite; flowering takes place long before leafing. The fruits are winged nuts.

The leaf buds of wych elm are situated at the end of the shoots, and are ovate and pointed. The flower buds, which are rather larger, grow lower down the stem, and are thick and round. Wych elm often has so many flower-buds that, after flowering, the branches appear lacking in leaves. The bud scales are covered with fine golden brown hairs.

The leaves, arranged in two rows, are short-stalked, large (3–6 in. long), pointed, and sharply and doubly serrated; the leaf bases are rather oblique. The upper-surfaces are as rough as sandpaper; the lower-surfaces are usually downy. It is not unusual on vigorous shoots of wych elm to see leaves which have three lobes at the apex; leaves

of this kind are not found in the two following species of elm. Often the lateral veins are forked. The leaves begin to unfold at the end of April.

The flowers, which come out at the beginning of March, form globular inflorescences, and very quickly develop fruits. The latter are large and green, and hang in thick clusters on the tree before the leaves have appeared. They ripen in June and the seed-vessels, which are then light brown, are dispersed in large numbers by the wind. If the fruits are sown when green, they germinate the same year; if sown when fully ripe, germination takes place the following spring. In wych elm the nut is situated in the centre of the winged fruit, and the small notch at the top of the wings does not extend to the nut.

Wych elm grows best on non-acid soils which are deep and rich, particularly if rich in nitrogen. It does not often give rise to sucker shoots from its roots during the lifetime of the main stem, but after that has died back, such shoots sometimes spring up and form fresh trees. Its valuable wood is tough, heavy, and can be cleft. The heartwood is brown, and the sapwood, which is often very wide, is lighter. The annual rings are very distinct. Elm wood is used principally in furniture-making, and for coffins.

There are a number of varieties of wych elm, including the variety *montana* which is commonly found in northern Scandinavia and has smaller leaves than the main species. In addition there are a number of garden forms with pendulous branches, or stiff upright habit, etc.

The distribution area of wych elm includes the greater part of Europe. In addition it is found in Asia. It is the commonest elm in Scotland, Wales, and northern England, and extends to hilly districts of the Midlands.

54. Smooth-Leaved Elm,
Ulmus carpinifolia

This elm is a typical representative of a group known as Field Elms, which are characteristic of the English lowlands. Their precise identification is difficult, even for the expert botanist.

This species usually has a straighter stem and a more continuous axis, and it appears to become a tree more quickly than wych elm, which may retain its bushy form for a longer time.

Smooth-leaved elm usually has smaller leaves than the wych elm, but their shape and size vary considerably. The leaves have stalks up to $\frac{1}{2}$ in. long and are smooth and shiny above (but rather rough in the case of stool shoots and epicormic branches); the lower surfaces are also glabrous or almost smooth.

The bases of the leaves are very oblique; the lateral veins are forked.

The young branches are almost glabrous, while the buds, which are smaller than those of wych elm, but have the same shape, are covered with white hairs.

A characteristic feature of this species and its allies is their ability to produce suckers and to spread in this way. In fact, along English hedgerows this is their usual method of reproduction. The development of cork ribs on shoots, especially the younger ones, is also typical.

The leaves both unfold and fall somewhat later than those of wych elm, and the autumn colouring is a beautiful yellow.

The fruits are a little smaller than those of the last species, and the nut is placed nearer the end of the wings, so that the notch extends down to the nut.

The wood of smooth-leaved elm is highly valued for furniture and coffin boards. It is very strong and tough, and impossible to cleave.

A common feature of the elms is their resistance to salt sea winds.

55. Fluttering Elm, *Ulmus laevis*

The name 'Fluttering Elm' comes from the German *Flatterulme* and refers to the flowers, which hang down on long stalks. The inflorescence resembles an umbel but has a more complicated structure.

The leaf-form of this elm closely resembles that of the last species, but the leaves have somewhat shorter stalks, and have characteristic curly hairs on the under-sides.

The lateral veins of the leaf are only occasionally forked. The leaf buds are slender and pointed, and the flower buds are very similar in form, but are a little thicker.

The bark of the stem is not so rough and cracked as that of the two last species; it falls off in thin, light grey flakes. Like smooth-leaved elm, this tree reproduces itself by suckers.

The flowers and the fruits have long stalks and thus differ from the other two elms. The fruits are small, with distinct marginal hairs on the wings and a relatively wide notch at the end.

The wood is not so valuable, as it is porous and has a very wide area of sapwood.

Fluttering elm is widely distributed across Europe, but is only grown as a specimen tree in Britain.

Berberis Family, Berberidaceae.

56. Barberry, *Berberis vulgaris*

The name 'barberry' comes from the learned writings of the Middle Ages (medical books from southern Italy) and probably originates from Arabic. The indigenous Welsh name of *eurdrain* signifies 'golden thorn', and refers to the golden blossoms and the spiny twigs.

Barberry is an attractive, thickly-branched bush about as high as a man. The branches are pendulous, glabrous, slightly furrowed and yellowish-grey. The shoot begins in a characteristic way in that all the leaves on the long shoots take the form of thorns (leaf thorns), each of which has 1–3 spikes. In the axils

of these thorns, short shoots develop, with broadly elliptical to ovate leaves, which have wavy and thorny margins and are arranged in bunches.

The flowers, which come out at the end of May, are yellow, with six sepals and six petals, and are grouped in clusters. They have a very insipid smell. The six stamens react to a stimulus of their filaments (by bees or a pencil) by quickly closing like a valve on the pistil, and depositing pollen on the visiting insect. In this way self-pollination is prevented.

The fruits are attractive red berries, which are oblong in shape; they contain pectin among other things and have an acid taste. In addition, the berries have a high content of Vitamin C.

Barberry is the alternate host plant for black rust, *Puccinia graminis*, a disease which attacks different kinds of corn, and may cause extensive damage with serious economic consequences. In Britain, where the barberry is scarce, black rust is never a severe threat to corn crops, but in Denmark, cultivation of barberry is forbidden.

Evidence of the parasitic fungus mentioned above appears on the leaves of barberry in May to June, in the form of dense orange spots called the 'summer spores'.

The wood of barberry is yellow and very hard, and is used occasionally for high quality decorative work. It contains, as do the bark and roots, a striking yellow substance which may be used for colouring wool and leather.

The natural range of this plant includes the greater part of Europe.

Currant Family, Ribesiaceae.

57. **Red Currant,** *Ribes rubrum*

The word 'currant' comes from *Corauntz*, an old English name for Corinth in Greece. True currants, or sun-dried grapes, were imported as 'raisins of Corauntz', and the name was later applied to the fruits of the wild bushes now to be described, which are quite unrelated in the botanical sense. The Danish name of *Ribs* and the Latin name *Ribes* both come from the German *Rebe*, signifying a vine.

The usual Welsh name for currants, *cyren*, is drawn from the English, e.g. *cyren goch* for red currant. But there is an older indigenous name of *rhyfon*. In Gaelic, currants are *dearc Fhrangach*, foreign berries.

The currant family contains a number of bushes which have alternate, palmately-lobed leaves. The flowers grow in clusters of five. The sepals, which are often coloured, are usually larger than the petals. The fruits are berries, and the pericarp is juicy.

The currant bushes that we know so well in gardens are the result of breeding and improvement, originally from various wild types with small and sour fruits.

The common features of these forms are that they are bushes 3–6 ft. high, which often spread by layering, i.e. the lowest branches touching the ground strike root. The winter buds are pointed and brown. The bark peels off the older branches in thin flakes. The leaves, which are serrated, have 3–5 pointed lobes, and are odourless.

The small hermaphrodite flowers grow in thick, drooping racemes. The sepals are greenish, brownish or reddish-brown, and are about twice as long as the yellowish petals.

The rather sour berries are usually red, but there are also cultivated types with whitish-yellow berries, called white currants. These fruits are used for syrup and jam.

Currant bushes are found growing wild in alder swamps and in thickets on soil which is not too dry.

The different types of currant bushes grow wild throughout Britain, and in north and north-east Europe, as far north as Lapland and Siberia.

58. Black Currant, *Ribes nigrum*

The name of this bush, which is a distinct species from the red currant, records the black colour of the fruit. The Welsh name is *cyren du*

The leaves of black currant have from three to five pointed lobes; their lower surfaces are covered with fine yellow glands, which have a characteristic smell.

The flowers, which are greenish on the outside and violet-red inside, are larger and more bell-shaped than those of red currant. There are also fewer flowers in the racemes. The berries are black, and have a characteristic taste. They have the same uses as red currants.

The buds are reddish-brown, rather plump, and have yellow glands like the leaves.

Black currant grows wild in scrub

areas and woodlands on damp ground, especially in alder swamps, where, as a result of the layering of branches, it spreads and forms small thickets.

Its range includes all Britain, and the European-Asiatic forest region from north-west France to Russia, the Caucasus, central Siberia and the greater part of Asia. In southern Europe it is found only as a cultivated plant.

59. Gooseberry, *Ribes uva-crispa*

Although the origin of the word 'gooseberry' is uncertain, it certainly has nothing to do with geese. It is most probably derived from the German *Kraussbeere*, meaning 'sour berry'. The Gaelic *groiseid* appears allied to the French *groseille*, while the Welsh *gwsber* has clearly come from the English. Another quaint Welsh name is *eirinen Fair*, the plum of St. Mary.

Wild gooseberry is a low bush with upright and arched branches. Unlike the other forms of *Ribes*, wild gooseberry has a single, or two- or three-pronged thorn growing on the

bark immediately below the leaves. The latter have from three to five wide lobes, and are somewhat smaller than the leaves of red currant and black currant. The leaves come out in April.

The flowers grow in clusters of one to three. Each flower is bell-shaped, and has a reddish calyx and a whitish-yellow corolla.

The berries are large, especially in the cultivated forms, and may be red, yellow or green. They may also be smooth, or have soft or stiff hairs. Syrup, jam, pies and jelly, etc. are made from these berries.

The common magpie moth, *Abraxis grossularia*, sometimes completely defoliates bushes, but only occasionally causes wide damage.

Wild gooseberry extends through Britain and Europe, with the exception of the southern regions and western Asia. It is difficult to determine its original range, as it has been cultivated since the Middle Ages and very easily becomes wild.

60. Alpine Currant, *Ribes alpinum*

This species is associated with mountains and northerly latitudes.

Alpine currant differs from the previous species in that it is dioecious.

The leaves are very small, three-lobed, and have shiny under-surfaces. The large, light, almost white buds are already fully developed in spring, and the leaves normally begin to appear as early as the second week of April.

The flowers are in erect racemes. Male racemes are thick and contain many flowers. Female racemes are open and have few flowers. Female flowers contain rudimentary stamens, and male flowers have rudimentary stigmas. The berries are red and tasteless.

As it comes into leaf so early, alpine currant is occasionally grown in hedges. It also tolerates shade and is sometimes used in gardens as a shrub for shady places where it is difficult for other plants to grow.

Alpine currant grows wild in Scotland and northern England, and throughout Europe, except for the Mediterranean region.

Rose Family, Rosaceae.

1. *Spiraea Group, Spiraeoideae.*

61. Willow-Leaved Spiraea,
Spiraea salicifolia

'Spiraea' is a well-known name of Greek and Latin extraction which now, in a botanical sense, only applies to the bush forms. This name is also used for other herbaceous perennials, *Filipendula, Aruncus* and *Astilbe*, all of them forms of meadow-sweet which belong to other genera. The word 'spiraea' alludes to the small fruits—slightly spiral and twisted—of the wild meadow-sweet.

Willow-leaved spiraea is a bush 3–6 ft. high, with upright, smooth, yellowish-brown branches which become greyish with age, and bark which peels off in thin strips. The leaves, which are about 3 in. long, are alternate, simple, lanceolate,

pinnately-veined and have serrated margins. The upper surfaces of the leaves are glabrous, while the midribs on the lower surfaces may be slightly hairy.

The flowers are small, with five light-red, or sometimes white, petals. They are grouped in narrow, thick, pinnacle-shaped inflorescences, which are situated at the end of the branches. The stamens are longer than the petals, and the fruits are multiple—the small fruits being capsules.

These shrubs are frequently used for boundary hedges and have spread and become wild in woods and thickets on damp ground. They are very liable to produce suckers. Rather a local shrub, the willow-leaved spiraea is commonest in North Wales. It was introduced from south-east Europe and Asia.

62. Sorbaria, *Sorbaria sorbifolia*

The name 'sorbaria' is derived from *sorbus* and refers to the similarity of the leaves to those of rowan (*Sorbus aucuparia*).

This thick and bushy shrub may be up to 5 ft. tall. It somewhat resembles willow-leaved spiraea, from which it differs in having pinnately compound leaves about a foot long,

composed of 13–23 lance-shaped serrated leaflets. The inflorescences are larger and more open than those of the spiraea. The shoots of the inflorescence have star-shaped hairs.

Sorbaria suckers freely, and as it is very hardy and thrives on poor soils, it has been occasionally used for hedges in exposed situations. Wild plants are found here and there, but they have spread from planted specimens.

It is native in northern Asia.

2. *Stone-fruit Group, Pomoideae.*

63. Cotoneaster,
Cotoneaster integerrima

The name 'cotoneaster' means 'wild quince'. It is a compound of Latin *cotonea*, quince, and *aster*, wild.

The native wild cotoneaster is a low bush with prostrate or upright branches. The leaves are alternate, oval and entire. The upper-surfaces are glabrous and dull dark green, and the under-surfaces are white- or grey-felted

The young branches are at first downy, but are later glabrous and reddish-brown. The small white or light-red flowers are in drooping racemes. The fruits are globular, about ¼ in. in diameter, red, and often have two stones.

This attractive shrub is found wild in Britain only on the lime-stone cliffs at the Great Orme's Head near Llandudno. Since that headland was named by the Vikings, the plant may have been brought from Scandinavia. Outside Scandinavia it is found in the greater part of Europe, and in Asia Minor.

The black-fruited cotoneaster, *Cotoneaster melanocarpa*, is a closely-related species which grows taller, and has more spreading branches. The leaves have fine hairs on the upper-surfaces, and are thickly felted on the under-surfaces. The inflorescences have four to seven flowers, and the fruits, when ripe, are black and full of bluish juice. It does not grow wild in Britain.

64. Snowy Mespilus,
Amelanchier spicata

Called 'snowy' from its showers of white blossom, and 'mespilus' from the German *Mispel*, a medlar.

Snowy mespilus is a shrub up to 12 ft. high with many stems and slender branches. The leaves are sparse and oval, with rounded base and short apex. The leaf margins are finely serrated. When young the leaves have some whitish down on the under-surfaces, but later they become more glabrous. The white flowers have very large corollas and form large racemes which are upright or projecting. Flowering, which takes place in May to June, is very abundant.

The fruits are round, about ½ in. in diameter, downy at the top and, when ripe, bluish-black. They contain a core with about ten seeds, and may be used for jam, etc.

Snowy mespilus is native to North America and has been introduced to Europe. In addition to being an attractive ornamental shrub it is tolerant and hardy, and is sometimes planted for decoration on the forest fringes.

65. Midland Hawthorn,
Crataegus oxyacanthoides

The name 'hawthorn' is explained under No. 66. This species is called 'Midland' because it is only really common in our Midland counties.

In its typical form the Midland hawthorn is a bush not more than 30 ft. high, and often has several stems. The leaves are somewhat jagged, obovate in outline, and the lowest lateral veins are extended forward. The upper leaf surface is dark green and rather shiny.

The flowers usually contain two, sometimes up to five, styles. The fruits when ripe are egg-shaped to round, with several stones, corresponding to the number of styles.

The sepals, which curve outwards, are plump and triangular.

This species comes into leaf at the end of April.

In England the Midland hawthorn is found wild in many places, but not on the poorer soils; it is most frequent in moist woodlands. It is not used so much for hedges as is the following species, common hawthorn.

Its range covers central and southern Europe.

66. Common Hawthorn,
Crataegus monogyna

The tree is probably named after its fruit, which is invariably called, in English country districts, a 'haw'.

Other common names are 'may', from the month of flowering, 'quickthorn' or 'quick' from the fast growth of young hedge plants, and 'whitethorn' from the colour of the blossom. (But see blackthorn, No. 82.) The Gaelic names are *draigh* and *sgitheach;* both these words mean 'thorn'. In Welsh, hawthorn is called *draen wen*, white thorn, and also *ysbyddad*.

The common hawthorn differs from the Midland variety in that it is usually a tree with a thickly-branched crown, and may occasionally reach a height of 60 ft. The branches are reddish-brown when young, but later become ash-grey. There are long shoots and short shoots, some of which develop reddish-brown thorns about ½ in. long. The buds are small and reddish, and the leaves unfold about one week later than those of the previous species.

The leaves are alternate and deeply laciniate to pinnatifid; a special feature is that the lower lateral veins are curved backwards. The upper-surfaces of the leaves are dull green;

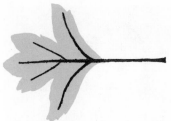

the lower-surfaces are often rather a bluish-green.

The half-umbellate inflorescences consist of a number of white flowers, each with five petals, borne on downy shoots. The flowers, which have a single style and usually 20 stamens, have a peculiar smell, rather like herrings, owing to the fact that they contain trimethylamine. Flowering takes place at the beginning of June and, as in the last species, is often very profuse.

The fruit, which is downy when young, is red, ovoid or globular, and has a single lemon-shaped stone. The stamens at the top of the fruit are short, plump and recurved.

There are several varieties of hawthorn, including the 'red thorn' often planted in gardens, pink forms, and forms with double flowers.

Both the hawthorns are common on grazing land, as the animals avoid these thorny bushes. At the same time, in these places, thornless trees and bushes often grow up in the shelter of the thorn trees, so that a single hawthorn bush in time can become the centre of a small thicket containing many different species of tree.

The wood of both the thorn species is hard, dense and heavy and is suitable for wood carving, but its main uses are firewood, hedge stakes, and cudgels.

Hawthorn is much used for hedges and windbreaks, and is very suitable for this purpose except on the poorest soils. The berries must be stored in moist sand for eighteen months before they will germinate. The young hedge plants need protecting with temporary fences for several years; nevertheless the thorn hedge remains our cheapest and best field boundary.

Hawthorn is common all over Britain, as well as in the rest of Europe. It also grows in North Africa and parts of Asia.

67. Mistletoe, *Viscum album*

The English name 'mistletoe', and the Danish and German name *Mistelten*, are derived from *mist*, which means manure, and the word *ten*, which here means (plant) shoot. We know from the old literature that in former times mistletoe was regarded as an unhealthy growth exuding or sweated out of the tree. Therefore the most likely explanation is that *mist* means, in addition to manure, an exudation or excrescence. The Welsh name is *uchelwydd*, upper tree, from its parasitic habit of growth on other trees. In Gaelic it is *an t'uil ioc*, that which heals all, a reference no doubt to its supposed supernatural powers.

Although mistletoe belongs to the natural family *Loranthaceae*, it is described here as it is often parasitic on the stems and branches of rowan, hawthorn and apple, and other trees in the *Pomoideae* group of the family *Rosaceae*.

Mistletoe is an evergreen shrub with green forked branches and yellowish-green leaves, which are opposite, narrow and leathery. The leaf bases are wedge-shaped.

This species is dioecious. The male flowers have 4–6 petals, while the female flowers have 4 petals. Flowering is in April to May, and

the flowers, which grow at the ends of the branches, are usually quite inconspicuous.

The fruits are whitish, rather shiny berries, with one or two seeds. The berries contain sticky juice which makes the seeds adhere to the beaks of the birds that eat them. The seeds are transferred to other branches and stems when the birds try to rid themselves of this sticky substance. This juice was formerly used for making birdlime.

When the seed germinates, it develops an embryonic stem which curves round and forms a connecting disk that grows into the tree's branch. From this connection, the characteristic roots of mistletoe penetrate in between the bark and wood of the branch.

There are three races of mistletoe. The first is parasitic on various broad-leaved trees (on a number of poplars, as well as on the species previously mentioned); the second on silver fir; the third on pine; but these last two are very rare in Britain. In Britain, mistletoe is rather infrequent, but further south, especially in France, it is very common, and may be harmful to the trees on which it is parasitic. However, the Normandy farmers find it a valuable crop, exporting it for Christmas decorations.

Mistletoe has been much associated with mythology and various superstitions, such as the ancient rites of the Welsh Druids. It has become our traditional decoration and 'kissing bough' at Christmas.

68. Rowan, *Sorbus aucuparia*

'Rowan' comes from Danish *Røn*, and is connected with the word 'rune', which suggests that the name could, perhaps, be translated 'magic tree'. In Scotland also the rowan was credited with magic powers, and was planted around every Highland croft to guard against witchcraft. The Gaelic name is *caorunn* and the Welsh name *cerddin*.

Mountain ash, from the shape of the leaves, is a common but misleading English name. This tree has no botanical connection with the common ash.

Rowan and the whitebeams are thornless trees or large bushes. The leaves are alternate and spirally arranged; the crown is composed of short and long shoots, with large winter buds. The flowers are white to whitish-yellow with five sepals and five petals, and form thick half-umbellate inflorescences composed of many flowers. They have a strong but unpleasant smell like those of hawthorn. The fruit is a berry-like pome and has a weak, often minute, core, with one seed in each compartment.

Rowan is normally a small tree, seldom exceeding 40 ft. in height, with pinnately compound leaves

consisting of 9–15 lance-shaped leaflets, which have sharply-serrated edges. The leaves unfold very early, sometimes in the middle of April. The autumn colours are yellow or red and the leaves fall not later than October. Flowering takes place at the end of May, and the fruits ripen in August. They are coral-red to orange, and usually contain three seeds. The fruits have a sour but pungent taste, and are frequently used for jelly. The seeds are widely dispersed by birds.

The annual shoots of rowan are brownish-violet or greyish-brown, with conspicuous lenticels. The buds are greyish or black to brown.

Rowan is a light-demander, but is very tolerant as regards soil conditions and is found in forest,

thicket and hedgerow. It grows throughout Britain, and reaches elevations of 2,000 ft. in Scotland. It grows wild in the rest of Europe, western Siberia and Asia Minor.

The wood is dense and hard, with light reddish sapwood and darker brownish heartwood. It is used especially for turnery and carving, tool handles, and farm implements.

69. Whitebeam, *Sorbus aria*

Whitebeam is so called because of the beautiful white colour of the under-side of its leaves, with 'beam', an Anglo-Saxon word for a tree.

Whitebeam is divided into several different races or varieties. The principal form, *Sorbus aria* (var. *typica*), is native to England, Wales, and Central Europe, and is often seen in hedgerows on chalk and limestone. It may be up to 60 ft. high, and has a rounded, thickly-leaved crown. The buds are brownish to pure green, on brown or green annual shoots. The leaves are simple without incisions, broadly elliptical or nearly round, and the undersurfaces are covered with snow-white down. The leaf margins are entire

near the base, sharply serrated above, and doubly serrated nearer the apex. The young shoots, and the branches of the inflorescences, are covered with thick white down.

The fruits vary in size from $\frac{1}{4} - \frac{1}{2}$ in. in diameter. They are more or

164

less dark red and often have many cork pores.

A variety of whitebeam, *Sorbus aria* var. *rupicola*, grows wild in northern England and Scotland, and also in Scandinavia. It can be distinguished from the main form by its spatulate, oblong leaves, with wedge-shaped entire bases. The leaves are coarsely toothed near the apex, with single to double serrations. The leaves are thick, and their upper-surfaces are shiny green, while the lower-surfaces are covered with thick greyish-white down.

The fruit is thicker than it is long, and has a length of about ½ in. It ripens at the end of October. The flesh of the fruit is yellow, mealy, and has no particular taste.

Like the following variety it is usually a stiffly branched bush 3–12 ft. high.

Another variety, *obtusifolia*, grows wild in Scandinavia, but only in a few places in Sweden and Norway. It differs from the preceding variety in its leaves, which have shorter stalks and are ovate-round with sharply serrated margins almost down to the leaf base. The undersides of the leaves are covered with lead-grey down, and the fruits are a little smaller. The similar variety *latifolia* is found in and around Devon, and in south-east Ireland.

70. Swedish Whitebeam,
Sorbus intermedia

Called 'Swedish' whitebeam, because it is more common in Sweden than elsewhere.

This species arose as a spontaneous hybrid, which has occurred many times, between rowan and whitebeam. The annual shoots are brown, often with one side greyish. The

buds are reddish to reddish-green, and the leaves are simple, ovate, pinnately lobed and serrated. The under-surfaces are grey-felted.

The flowers are rather larger than those of rowan, and the fruits are longer, orange-red, and have scattered, fine lenticels. The fruits ripen in September; they have a rather sweet taste and usually contain two pips.

If the seed of a Swedish whitebeam is sown the seedlings will be very uniform and will appear identical with the mother tree. This is because the Swedish whitebeam is an 'apomict', i.e. seed is produced vegetatively without cross-pollination, and therefore the parent tree is reproduced unchanged. This has a special significance in the case of trees with particularly valuable characteristics. It is only necessary to find an outstandingly good individual and collect seed from it, and one can be sure that the progeny will be equally promising. In Britain, Swedish whitebeam is grown only as a decorative tree. It shows remarkable resistance to town smoke, and grows well even in the heart of Glasgow.

Swedish whitebeam may be a large tree up to 60 ft. tall and 12 ft. in girth. The wood is whitish, tough and difficult to cleave; there is no distinct heartwood. It is very suitable for making rulers and is the best wood for skittles and wooden balls. It is used for artists' instruments, turnery and wood carving.

The natural range of this species is limited to southern Sweden, Bornholm, Åland and Åbo in Finland, the Baltic, and north-east Germany. Very similar varieties are found in Scotland and Norway.

71. Finnish Whitebeam,
Sorbus hybrida

The recognized name of this species is due to the fact that it grows primarily in Finland.

This species, like Swedish whitebeam, appears to be a hybrid between rowan and common whitebeam—closely related to the variety *rupicola*. It has reddish-brown buds, and the annual shoot often has distinct light cork pores (lenticels).

The leaf, which differs clearly from that of the other whitebeams, has 1–3 pairs of free lobes, while the

rest of the leaf blade is sub-pinnate to pinnately-lobed, with a coarsely serrated margin. The under-surface of the leaf is light grey-felted.

Finnish whitebeam has a thick round crown and resembles Swedish whitebeam, but it is a smaller tree, only 12–13 ft. high.

Finnish whitebeam flowers a few days earlier than Swedish whitebeam, and usually has many flowers in very thick inflorescences. The fruits are globular, about ½ in. thick, and bright red in colour. They ripen in the middle of August, and have a bitter-sweet taste which makes them very suitable for jam.

This tree has a very limited range, which includes only the coastal regions of the Scandinavian countries, excluding Denmark; and also, remarkably, the Scottish island of Arran, to which point the Vikings possibly brought the seeds.

72. Wild Service Tree,
Sorbus torminalis

The wild service tree is a plant which has been known from ancient times. The medicinal effect of the berries was known to the Romans. According to Pliny the plant provides a good remedy—even if *tantum probabile*—for colic and dysentery. Both the Danish name *Tarmvrid* and the Latin specific name *torminalis* refer to these medicinal properties. (*Tarm*, intestine; *vrid*, writhe.) 'Service' is adapted through Anglo-Saxon *syrfe* from Latin *sorbea* and *sorbus*, and 'wild' is added to distinguish it from the garden service tree, *Sorbus domestica*. Another old, unexplained, name is 'chequers tree'.

Wild service differs considerably from the other species in this group. It is a bush or small tree with plump shiny green buds. The leaves are

wide, with 5–7 pointed lobes, downy when young, later glabrous. The lowest pair of lobes are projecting and large. The autumn colour of the leaves is blood red.

The flowers are white, and are situated in open inflorescences. The fruit is round or oval, about ½ in. long; when ripe it is leathery brown and dotted with cork pores. The taste is sourish, but when fully ripe they are sweet enough to be eaten raw; they were once sold in Kentish markets, as 'chequer-berries'.

Wild service is a southern and central European species found in Kent and adjoining English counties, but it is rare. It also extends into North Africa, the Caucasus, Asia Minor and Syria.

73. Crab Apple, *Malus sylvestris*

'Crab' comes to us from Scottish 'scrab' and Norse *Krab*, while 'Apple' and the Danish *Abild* and *Aeble* are variants of another name, known in different forms throughout the greater part of northern and central Europe. However, the meaning of this name is uncertain. The Welsh *afal* and Gaelic *ubhall* stem from Norse roots.

Crab apple seldom grows taller than 20 ft., and often takes the form of a large bush. The crown is thickly branched and consists of long shoots and short shoots. Some of the short shoots, when the terminal bud falls away, develop into thorns. The leaves are alternate, ovate to

broadly elliptical, short-pointed and serrated. The leaf stalk is about half as long as the leaf blade. The leaves, young shoots and buds are all glabrous or only very slightly hairy.

Wild crab comes into leaf in late April and flowering usually takes place in early May. The sweet-scented flowers grow at the end of the short shoots, and form umbel-like inflorescences of a few flowers. The petals are about an inch long, reddish on the outside and white on the inside. There are large numbers of yellow anthers.

The apples are borne on very long stalks and are small—usually only an inch or so in diameter—almost globular and greenish-yellow, occasionally with a reddish tinge on one side. They are very sour indeed, but nevertheless they are the ancestors of many of our cultivated types. Alone, or mixed with rowan berries, crab apples make excellent jelly.

Wild crab now grows wild over the whole of Europe, but it is difficult to know where it was originally native. It seems to have been cultivated to some extent long ago and to have spread from this source as a wild tree.

The sapwood is light red and the heartwood is reddish-brown. The wood is hard, heavy and strong and is used for wooden screws, cam wheels, mallets and wood-carving, etc.

Downy crab apple

The downy crab apple, *Malus pumila*, which frequently occurs as a wild tree, resembles the common crab apple, but has shorter leaf-stalks, while the leaves, shoots and buds are hairy to grey-felted. The fruits are slightly larger and not so sour.

Crab apple

Wild pear

74. **Wild Pear**, *Pyrus communis*

The English 'pear' and the Danish *Paere* are connected with the Latin *pyrus* (*pirus*), the meaning of which is unknown. A number of corresponding names in other European languages come from the same root as *pirus*, such as the German *Birne* and the French *poire*. The Welsh name of *gellyg* shows no relation, however, to the Latin *pirus*, and may indicate that this tree is truly native to Wales. In Gaelic it is called *peur*, and also *meas araidh*, meaning 'remarkable fruit'.

There are several different forms of pears: the primitive types with small fruits and the improved cultivated varieties with large fruits such as 'Bonne Louise' and 'Conference'.

The wild form of pear, *Pyrus communis*, is found here and there growing wild. It differs from wild crab in having a more open crown with one continuous main stem (or several continuous stems), and in the conical (not hollowed) base of the fruit. The young shoots are light grey to brownish, and have spines sometimes up to more than an inch long. The buds are grey.

The leaves have long stalks, the leaf stalk being approximately the same length as the leaf blade, which in this variety is small, almost circular and short-pointed.

The flowers are white with red anthers, and grow in strongly umbellate inflorescences of up to nine flowers. They have an unpleasant smell.

The fruits are small and almost globular; before ripening they have a sour and astringent taste. When ripe they become yellow and sweet-scented, but they remain ripe only for a short time, and quickly become rotten.

Wild pear suckers freely and can form small thickets in this way. It grows wild in central and eastern Europe, and in western Asia.

3. *Rose Group, Rosoideae.*

75. **Raspberry,** *Rubus idaeus*

'Raspberry' signifies 'rough berry', and is no doubt based on the uneven surface of the composite fruit. The older name of 'hindberry', still used in Scotland, comes from Danish *Hindbaer*. The word 'hind' has developed from the root *km* (represented in Greek by *kemas*, a female deer without horns). As there is also another root *kem* with the meaning 'arched' or 'covering' this may have developed into a word which gradually came to mean arched, surrounded or encased. Such a word may probably be the basis of *Hindbaer*, which in this case would mean 'arched berry', a very suitable name for the hat-like, easily detached 'berry' which, before being picked, encases the white conical receptacle. The Welsh name is *mafonwydd*; the Gaelic names of *sugh-chraobh* and *suibheag* signify 'juicy bush'.

Raspberry has a perennial rootstock, but the shoots are biennial, that is, the single shoots are never more than two years old.

The one-year-old shoots are herbaceous and without flowers. The second-year shoots are woody, covered with fine, somewhat sharp bristles, and they bear flowers and fruits. These second-year shoots die during the winter after they have borne fruit.

The leaves are pinnately compound with 3-7 leaflets, and are white-felted underneath.

The flowers, which appear in June, are small and have narrow white petals and many stamens. There are a number of styles, equivalent to the portions of the fruit which is about to set.

The fruit is a compound berry consisting of small drupes (drupels) united round a cone-shaped flower receptacle. When the fruits or berries are ripe they are detached from the receptacles, which, however, remain on the plant. Raspberries are generally red, but there are also yellow forms. It is a very important berry-bearing fruit of which there are several cultivated types. The main commercial growing region lies on the southern fringe of the Scottish Highlands, around Blairgowrie.

As a wild plant raspberry is common in the forests and woods of Scotland, Northern England and Scandinavia, especially on the drier soils. In forest clearings it grows freely on nitrogen-rich ground, forming large thickets which are extended every year by suckers and by seeding. Birds assist in the dispersal of seed.

Raspberry grows wild not only in Britain and Scandinavia, but throughout Europe, in the greater part of Asia, and in North America.

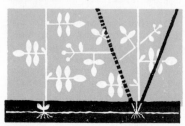

First-year shoot (white). Second-year shoot (black dotted line). Dead shoot (black).

76. **Blackberry,** *Rubus fruticosus*

'Blackberry', from the colour of the ripe fruit, explains itself. Both the plant and the fruit are also known, especially in Scotland, as 'bramble', a name allied to the Danish *Brombaer*.

The first part of the name 'bramble' seems to mean 'thorny plant'. It is related to the old High German *brama*, thorn bush, and the Anglo-Saxon *bremel* or *braembel*, a *Rubus* species with thorns. The Welsh name is *miar*. Gaelic names are *dris* and *droigheann*, which refer to the thorns, and *lus nan dearc*, herb of the berries.

There are many closely related sub-species of blackberry which can only be identified by the specialist. The wild forms are common weeds of woodland and hedgerow; cultivated strains are grown in gardens for their luscious fruit, and also in commercial orchards.

Blackberry differs from raspberry in having very prickly, arched or prostrate stems, the extremities of which often strike root and form new plants. The first-year shoots, which do not bear flowers, usually have compound leaves with five leaflets each. In the axils of these leaves, short flower-bearing side shoots with compound leaves, comprised of only three leaflets, appear in the second year. After the fruit has ripened the second-year shoots die.

First-year shoot (white). Second-year shoot (black dotted line). Dead shoot (black).

The compound leaves have long stipules, and the serrated leaflets are usually white or grey-felted on the under-surfaces. They may remain green in the winter.

The flowers are larger than those of raspberry, and have white or pink petals. The fruit is a compound berry consisting of a number of small carpels known as drupels. After ripening, the fruit is not released from the dome-shaped flower receptacle, but (if not eaten by the birds) falls together with it. The berries are at first green, then red, and finally black. When ripe they are aromatic and have a pleasant taste.

Blackberry grows wild throughout the British Isles and is widely spread in central Europe.

77. Dewberry, *Rubus caesius*

The derivation of 'dewberry' is uncertain; it may be related to atmospheric 'dew'; or to the Gaelic *dhu*, meaning black; or to the common occurrence of two carpels, hence 'two-berry'. All alike fit this quaint plant. Dewberry has only a few carpels in each compound fruit; there may indeed be only two, or even one, from each flower. The appearance of two carpels together, each containing a seed, suggested to imaginative country people the comparison with the scrotum and two testicles of a male animal. The Danish name *Korbaer* is related to the Swedish dialect word, *kodden* (*Rubus saxatilis* or stone bramble) and with the Danish word *Kodde* (English 'cod'), which mean the testicles or scrotum of a male animal.

Dewberry is closely related to blackberry, but has a less vigorous and lower growth habit. The stalks are round, glaucous, and have weak, short and bristle-like, prickles. The compound leaves always consist of three leaflets and these leaflets are often lobed

There are a few white flowers in each inflorescence. The fruit, which usually consists of very large carpels, is covered with a glaucous bloom and has a flat insipid taste.

Dewberry grows wild throughout the greater part of Europe, and in Asia and Siberia.

78. Dog Rose, *Rosa canina*

The name 'rose' is of Latin origin, but the meaning is not known. It was adopted in early popular English and was used with the meaning of a conspicuous and beautiful flower. The word 'dog' in this connection has a disparaging meaning and indicates 'worthless in comparison with cultivated roses'.

The origin of 'hip' for the characteristic compound fruit is not clear. The explanation is made more difficult by the fact that originally the word did not refer only to the fruit, but to the whole bush.

The Welsh for 'rose' is *rhosyn*, and the wild rose is *rhosyn gwyllt*. The usual Gaelic name is *ros*, but there is also an old name of *drisbhil*, which means the 'thorn-fringed' (bush).

The roses are bushes which have sharp prickles and frequently produce suckers. The leaves are alternate, spirally arranged and pinnately compound, with several elliptical and serrated leaflets. The flowers have five petals.

The hip, sometimes called a false fruit, consists of an urn-shaped (flower) receptacle. When the flesh is ripe the hip is usually red in colour; inside there are many carpels which each become a small nut covered with fine brittle hairs.

There are many different forms of dog roses, which are difficult to distinguish from each other. They are bushes 3–10 ft. high, with vigorous arched and erect shoots, armed with strong sickle-shaped prickles, with the help of which the plant can climb upwards on the neighbouring trees and bushes.

The leaves are pinnately compound, with 5–7 sharply serrated, glabrous or slightly hairy, leaflets.

The long-stalked flowers, which grow in groups, are pale pink to white, with laciniate, recurved and tapering sepals.

The hips are oval to egg-shaped and ripen late. Like all hips, those of the dog rose are rich in vitamin C.

Dog rose may reach a stem diameter of about one foot. However, the wood known in commerce as 'rosewood' comes from various tropical trees, and *never* from the rose species.

The dog rose is common on woodland fringes and along the hedgerows and boundaries of commons and other grazing land.

79. Scotch Rose, Burnet Rose, *Rosa spinosissima*

Called 'Scotch' rose from its frequency in Scotland, and 'burnet' rose from the resemblance of its leaves to those of the herb burnet, *Poterium officinale*. This herb in turn gets its name from old French *burnete* or *brunette*, because its leaves are often a deep reddish-brown.

Scotch rose is one of our most beautiful roses, and gives colour to the grey sand dunes. It produces suckers and often forms small thickets in this way. This rose is an easily recognizable bush up to 3 ft. high, with thickly-branched dark-brown shoots which are densely studded with straight prickles and bristles.

The leaves are small, with 5–11 leaflets which are broadly elliptical, sometimes almost circular, dull green and simply serrated.

The flowers are very large, creamy-white, and have a pleasant scent. The hips are almost globular, blackish-red when ripe, and not more than ½ in. in diameter.

This species is wild in scattered localities in central and southern Europe, and in Asia from Asia Minor and the Caucasus to Siberia. Finally it occurs in Manchuria and north-west China.

80. Ramanas Rose, *Rosa rugosa*

The origin of the word 'ramanas' is unrecorded. The Danish name *Rynket Rose* refers to the leaves which are apparently wrinkled. This is a translation from the Latin specific name, which forms the direct basis for the frequently used name 'rugosa rose'. The name 'Kamtschatka rose' refers to the variety *Rosa rugosa kamtschatica*, a scarce northern variety, but is often used as being synonymous with ramanas rose.

Ramanas rose can be easily distinguished from other roses by the stout leaves composed of 7–9 dark-green, wrinkled leaflets, and by the hairy shoots which are thickly covered with pointed and straight prickles, and with bristles. The flowers are large, light reddish-violet, or pure white. The hips are large, fleshy and flatly-globular, and have a high content of vitamin C.

The bush grows to a height of 3–6 ft., and rapidly spreads by means of suckers.

The area of its natural distribution extends from southern Kamtschatka to Korea, northern China and Japan—regions where the winter temperatures often fall to zero. Ramanas rose is a typical coast plant and as such is extremely hardy both in Britain and in Scandinavia.

This rose was introduced to Europe in the middle of the last century. It was later discovered that it was extraordinarily tolerant of varied soil conditions and would grow equally well on lime-rich clays and the poorest sandy and stony coastal areas. It also proved resistant to winds and sea fogs, and has been widely planted along our coasts.

Under cultivation, ramanas rose has given rise to a number of beautiful hybrid forms, which show its distinctive violet-red coloration.

81. Sweet Briar, Eglantine, *Rosa eglanteria*

Called 'sweet' from its fragrant foliage, and 'briar' or 'brier' from an Anglo-Saxon word meaning a thorny bush (cf. bramble, No. 76). 'Eglantine' is derived, through French *aiglant*, from the Latin *aculentus*, and signifies prickly.

Sweet briar somewhat resembles dog rose (No. 78), but has a stiffer and more upright growth habit. The branches have very strong, sickle-shaped prickles, but there are also here and there small straight, or almost straight, bristle-like prickles.

The compound leaves have 7–9 leaflets, which are oval or almost circular, doubly serrated and with rounded bases. The edges and under-surfaces of the leaflets are nearly always covered with glands, which have the scent of apples or grapes. The scent is particularly noticeable when a leaf is rubbed.

The flower stalks are short and have both glands and stiff hairs. The flower is dark pink, even darker than that of the dog rose. The hips are about half an inch long, and often have glandular hairs and bristles.

Sweet briar grows in hedges and on dry hillsides, and is one of the roses most frequently used for planting rose hedges. It is common throughout the British Isles, and is distributed throughout the greater part of Europe. It is a parent of many fine garden hybrid briars.

82. Blackthorn, Sloe,
Prunus spinosa

Called 'blackthorn' by reason of its black bark, and to distinguish it from whitethorn or hawthorn (Nos. 65 and 66); the flowers of all, however, are white. The name 'sloe', or in Scotland, 'slae', is usually derived from the fruit. 'Sloe', and the Danish *Slåen*, are, however, of uncertain derivation.

In Wales, this tree is called *draen ddu*, black thorn; but the Welsh name for plum fruit is *eirin*. In Irish Gaelic the blackthorn is called *draigean dub*, black thorn. But the Scots Gaelic name is *buileastair*, from bullace (see No. 83), which gives rise to a Scots name of 'bullister'.

On cliffs along the coast, on dry hills, on the edge of forests and in hedges, blackthorn forms a dense and, at the time of flowering, beautiful growth.

Blackthorn grows 3–10 ft. high and is a thorny bush, thickly branched from the ground. The thorns are modified branches which are woody and have buds and leaves. The young branches are covered with fine downy hairs. The leaves, which are alternate, are very small, serrated and broadly lance-shaped.

The white flowers, with five petals, usually bloom in vast quantities in March or April, often *before*, but in some years not until *after*, the bush comes into leaf. They grow both on the short shoots, where there may be many flower buds, and on the long shoots, where the flower buds are situated on each side of the central leaf buds.

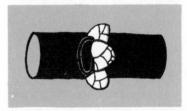

Only one flower is produced from each flower bud, and the flower stalks are glabrous. In one variety (var. *coetanea*) the flowers always appear at the same time as the leaves, and these flowers are usually larger than the common form.

The fruits, which are drupes, are erect, round, with a bluish bloom, and up to half an inch in diameter. They contain tannin, which gives them an astringent taste; however, this diminishes noticeably if the fruits have been frosted. The fruit stones are round, sometimes ellipsoidal and usually somewhat compressed. Sloes are still used in the preparation of sloe gin.

Blackthorn is liable to produce a vast number of suckers. In this way a single bush can in time develop into a small thicket, which is in fact the extension of one individual. As a result of this characteristic, blackthorn is not suitable for field hedges, as it may easily spread on to the adjoining land.

The impenetrable scrub formed by blackthorn bushes provides cover for many birds and is the favourite haunt of shrikes. On grazing lands blackthorn often protects various encroaching young broad-leaved trees from grazing animals.

Blackthorn is found wild all over the British Isles. It grows wild throughout Europe except for the most northerly regions.

83. Bullace, *Prunus insititia*

'Bullace' is derived from the old French name *béloce*.

Bullace resembles blackthorn, but is larger and may sometimes be a small tree. It has larger flowers, and usually two or more come from each flower bud. The flower stalks are hairy. The pendulous fruits are larger than those of blackthorn, bluish-black or sometimes yellow, and have a pleasant taste. The stones are more elongated, sharply-edged, and resemble small plum stones. The leaves are broadly elliptical, downy on the under-surfaces, and somewhat larger than those of blackthorn. The young branches have velvety hairs of uneven length.

Bullace lacks fully-developed spines, but instead the short shoots often degenerate and produce a type of thorn (or false spine).

Varieties of bullace include the true Mirabelle Plum (*Prunus insititia* var. *syriaca*) which has small yellow fruits, and the Reine Claude (*Prunus insititia* var. *italica*). In addition bullace is the parent stock of many other cultivated plums.

Except in the south and Midlands, bullace is seldom a wild tree, but here and there one is found—apparently an escape from former cultivation—on the edges of woodlands and in hedges where, like blackthorn, it may spread by means of suckers and form thick groups.

It hybridizes easily with blackthorn and it is open to question whether many of our most beautiful blackthorn bushes are not in fact intermediate forms.

84. Wild Cherry, Gean,
Prunus avium

The English 'cherry', the French *cerise*, the Gaelic *sirist*, and Welsh *ceirios*, have the same root in the Latin *cerasus*, the meaning of which is unknown, as is the origin of 'gean', used chiefly in Scotland. The German name, *Kirsche*, is also applied to cherry brandy.

In woodlands wild cherry may be a tree up to 102 ft. high, with sturdy branches which project upwards. In young trees the branching is regular, with a main axis and side branches arranged in whorls, but when old it loses this form to some extent.

The bark is greyish-brown, and is smooth and shiny in youth, but with age it develops a peculiar ragged appearance, due to portions becoming rough and breaking off horizontally. It may be easily recognized by the lenticels which form horizontal stripes.

The leaves are elliptical, doubly serrated and downy on the under-surfaces. The leaf stalk has two red, or sometimes yellow, glands.

The beautiful snow-white flowers, with five petals, unfold in May, when leafing begins. They come from special buds, both on the long shoots and on the short shoots, which contain only flowers.

The fruit of wild cherry is a blackish-red drupe with a smooth, almost globular, stone. These fruits are very small and have a pleasant taste, but are not so juicy as the many cultivated types. Forms of this species growing wild, but having perhaps originated from gardens, are sometimes found with dark red, light red, and also light yellow and whitish-yellow cherries. The seeds are widely dispersed by both man and bird.

The wood is hard, with pale reddish sapwood and reddish-yellow to light reddish-brown heartwood, which with age becomes dark reddish-brown. It looks something like mahogany, and is very valuable for the finer types of cabinet-making. It is also used for turnery and carving, and for instrument-making.

Wild cherry is common throughout Britain, especially on the chalk downs of the south. It is widely distributed in Europe, with the exception of the extreme north, and also occurs in western Asia.

A remarkable feature of this and other cherries is the outflow of a sweet, yellowish-brown resin, from any wound in the living wood. This is called a 'gum flood', and its purpose is apparently to ward off insects or fungal diseases. The same resin occurs in the fruits.

85. Dwarf Cherry, *Prunus cerasus*

The name 'morello', sometimes applied to dwarf cherry, is normally used for certain cultivated forms. Morello appears to have come from the mediaeval Latin *amarella*, which in turn is derived from *amarus*, bitter. However, dwarf cherries have a sour rather than a bitter taste.

Dwarf cherry has quite a different branching habit from wild cherry (No. 84) as the branches are thinner, supple and overhanging. In addition the growth is lower, and the branching more irregular.

The leaves are smaller than those of wild cherry, and are glabrous on both sides. The glands, which are less conspicuous, are situated on the leaf *base* and not on the actual leaf *stalk*.

The flowers unfold later than the leaves, and it is a feature of dwarf cherry that the flower buds also produce the leaves.

The fruits are sour, dark red, and in the cultivated forms are rather large (see colour plate, p. 83). They are used to a considerable extent in jam, syrup, liqueurs, etc.

Dwarf cherry spreads more quickly than wild cherry, by means of suckers, and in this way often forms small thickets. The amygdalin content of the bark is not so high, and the taste is therefore less bitter.

This tree is native in England, and has also 'escaped' from cultivation in many places where conditions favour its growth.

86. Cherry Plum, *Prunus cerasifera*

The English name signifies that this species is a plum which bears fruit resembling cherries in shape and size. The alternative 'myrobalan' comes from an old name originally used for various fruits from the southern countries which were used for ointments. The Greek word *myron* means sweet-scented ointment, and *balanos* is a fruit such as an acorn or date.

The name 'mirabel' is also applied to certain varieties of cherry plum, and is derived from Latin *mirabilis*, admirable.

Cherry plum may be a small tree or a large bush up to 25 ft. high. Unlike blackthorn it has completely smooth branches, and the young shoots are often 'verdigris' green on the shaded sides. The leaves are narrowly ovate and comparatively small. The flower buds on the long shoots are situated on either side of a leaf bud, and each one seldom contains more than a single flower.

The flowers are pure white, rather larger than those of blackthorn; they bloom in April to May before the leaves unfold. The fruits, which are drupes, are very large, round, pendulous, and yellow or red in colour. They have a pleasant taste and are often produced in large quantities.

Cherry plum sometimes bears spines, but they are not nearly so numerous, nor so closely spaced, as those of blackthorn.

Some of our cultivated plums are considered to be hybrids between blackthorn and cherry plum. The well-known copper-leaved plum is a variety, *pissardii*, of this species.

In situations which are not too exposed, cherry plum is a suitable plant for hedges, as it does not have the annoying habit of producing numerous suckers.

87. Bird Cherry, *Prunus padus*

Called 'bird' cherry because its small fruits attract only the birds. In Scotland it is called 'hag' cherry and the fruits are 'hags'.

Bird cherry may be either a large bush or a small tree up to 45 ft. high. The branches are reddish-brown, with light brown spots due to the scattered lenticels. The winter buds are slender and pointed. The dull green leaves are 2–5 in. long, oval, somewhat wrinkled and finely serrated. There are usually two glands at the top of the leaf stalk.

It can be clearly seen that the lateral veins on the under-side run sharply forward, and, just inside the leaf margin, are connected to each other by cross veins. This characteristic ribbing is found in other woody plants such as wild cherry and dwarf cherry, but in these it is less distinct.

Bird cherry flowers in May, with white, strongly sweet-scented blooms in long drooping racemes. The flowers are pollinated by various insects, especially bees and flies.

The small black fruits are drupes. Owing to their content of tannin they have an astringent taste. The stones are oval, pointed, and have a distinct, but irregular, crest.

Both the bark and the wood contain amygdalin, and, when freshly broken, they have a very unpleasant smell.

The wood is composed of light sapwood and darker yellowish-brown heartwood. It can be used for woodwork, but has no particular value or special use. The young stems and branches are tough and have therefore been used for barrel bands and cooperage rings.

In Britain the bird cherry is distinctly a highland tree. It is common in the Scottish glens, some valleys in northern England, and in mid-Wales, but is scarce or unknown elsewhere, except under cultivation.

The distribution of this species includes Europe to northern Spain and Italy, Asia Minor, the Caucasus, northern Asia, north China, Korea and Kamtschatka.

88. Rum Cherry, *Prunus serotina*

The name 'rum' cherry refers to the aromatic scent of the blossom.

Rum cherry is closely related to the last species, but has a taller and more upright growth habit. The leaves show the difference more clearly, as they are narrower, glossy and finely serrated; the upper-surfaces are dark green and the under-surfaces light green. The bridging cross-veins, described under bird cherry, are absent from rum cherry.

The white flowers are smaller, and the racemes are upright at the time of flowering.

The fruits, which are berry-like drupes, are blackish-red, and ripen late in the year. The calyx (cup) is permanent, and looks like a small collar at the base of the fruit. The fruit stone is nearly smooth. On the whole, this species is late in leafing, flowering and leaf fall.

Rum cherry is indigenous to the eastern part of North America, where it may reach heights of up to 90 ft. It was first introduced to Europe as an ornamental tree in parks and gardens. It is also used for hedge planting on poor soils.

The wood is very hard, and has a light yellowish-brown sapwood and an attractive reddish-brown heartwood, which looks rather like mahogany. It is a valuable wood for high quality furniture, etc., in America, where the large dimensions needed can be obtained.

89. St Lucie Cherry,
Prunus mahaleb

The name 'St Lucie' is from the French *bois de St Lucie*, and refers to the odorous wood.

St Lucie cherry is usually a bush, but under favourable circumstances may be a tree up to 30 ft. in height. It is strongly branched, with wide-spreading branches. The youngest shoots are light grey, rather sticky with glandular hairs, and finely grey-felted, later becoming brownish. A typical feature is that numerous light grey, almost white, lenticels give the branches a spotted appearance.

The leaves are glabrous, glossy, 1–2 in. long, ovate to circular, and abruptly pointed. The sweet-scented

white flowers grow in groups of 4–12, forming small racemes. The fruit is black when ripe, and has a smooth stone.

The bark and wood contain coumarin which has a very pleasant smell. The special flavour which is given to tobacco in the well-known cherry-wood pipes—made from St Lucie cherry—is due to coumarin.

St Lucie cherry grows wild in southern Europe and the East, but is cultivated outside these regions as an ornamental shrub.

Peaflower Family, Papilionaceae.

90. Robinia, False Acacia,
Locust, *Robinia pseudoacacia*

'Robinia' is the same as the Latin name given in honour of Robin, the French gardener who planted the first specimens introduced into Europe from America, in about 1600. The name 'False Acacia' indicates that this species, like many true acacias, has thorns, and furthermore that it has seed pods and pinnately compound leaves. 'Locust' arises from confusion with the true locust tree of the Near East, *Ceratonia siliqua*, which yields the carob beans or locusts that nourished John the Baptist in the wilderness; the seed pods of the robinia are somewhat similar.

This tree may be easily recognized at a distance by its characteristic domed crown, which is loosely composed of irregular branches. It grows up to 90 ft. high.

The branches are smooth, and have stipular spines. (Stipules are usually small leaves growing each side of the base of the leaf stalk; stipular spines are stipules which have developed into thorns.) These thorns are strongest on the young shoots. On branches in the crown of the tree they are weak, or may be absent.

The buds of robinia are difficult to see, as they are almost completely sunk in the branches between the stipular spines. The bark is rough and rugged, deeply marked with irregular furrows.

The leaves unfold late in the season, in the latter half of May. They are pinnately compound, with 7–19 oval leaflets, which are fresh green on the upper-surfaces and bluish-green on the under-surfaces.

The typical white 'peaflowers' are contained in drooping racemes 4–8 in. long. They are sweet-smelling and contain much nectar, and are therefore frequently visited by bees.

The fruits are glabrous pods 2–4 in. long. When ripe they become dark greyish-brown, and they remain in position until far on into the winter. The pods contain up to ten small, very hard seeds.

Robinia has a most distinctive wood. The sapwood is very narrow, light yellow, and consists of 2–3, occasionally 4, annual rings. The heartwood is hard, golden to yellowish-brown or greenish-yellow in colour, and shows clear annual rings and a 'flame' structure. The wood is very strong and extremely durable; it is especially suitable for fencing stakes or posts, mining timber, etc. It is also used to a limited extent in furniture-making and turnery.

Robinia comes from eastern North America. It was introduced to Europe at the start of the seventeenth century as one of the first American tree species, and great hopes were placed on it as a forest tree. These hopes have only been realized in the Balkans, and especially in Hungary, where false acacia has been successfully established on large areas of the plains.

In Britain and also in Scandinavia, especially in Denmark, robinia has been experimentally used as a forest tree, particularly on poor soils where it can grow well, since its roots are able to form bacterial nodules, with the help of which it is able to utilize the air's free nitrogen. For example, it is a useful tree for screening old colliery tips.

However, it has now been almost abandoned as a timber tree, largely because it does not, with us, produce sufficiently large and straight stems. On the other hand, robinia is a graceful, ornamental tree.

M

178

91. Broom, *Sarothamnus scoparius*

'Broom' comes from Anglo-Saxon *brom*, and denotes the use of the whip-like twigs.

The Welsh name is *banadl*, and the Gaelic, *bealaidh*.

In our climate broom—although it is often lower—may reach a height of 10 ft. The branches are green, twig-like, and have five wings or

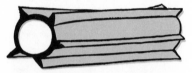

ribs. The leaves, which are comparatively sparse, have either three leaflets or else are simple and entire. They often fall early in the year, and therefore the plant depends to a great extent on the green branches for the assimilation of carbon dioxide from the air.

The large, bright yellow flowers appear in considerable numbers in May and June. Each flower contains five short stamens, five long stamens, and a long style. The long stamens and style lie closely within the typical corolla of petals of the pea family. The flowers can only be pollinated by large insects. At the first visit, the weight of the insect causes the release of both sorts of stamens—which with great force deposit their pollen on to the insect —and also of the style, whose stigma catches any pollen already hanging on the insect.

The fruits are large, flat, hairy pods, which are black when ripe. They open with a sharp, clearly audible crack, and seeds shoot out from them. The seeds have a small juicy appendage which is a favourite food of ants; the seeds are therefore widely dispersed by these insects.

Like many other species in the pea family, common broom has a 'hard' seed. This means that in a certain proportion of the seeds the shell is for varying periods impervious to the water necessary for germination. If the seed is only lightly rubbed with sandpaper, or boiled for quite a short time, the hardness is removed, and it will germinate immediately after sowing. However, the hard shell has a well-established function. In nature, some of the seeds germinate while others remain viable until the shell is broken, which may take from one to, occasionally, ten years. These hard seeds are, therefore, the reason why common broom grows so freely in northern countries where, in most years, it is partly frozen and sometimes completely killed by the cold. This bush would therefore disappear after a time if it were not for the fact that the seeds are able to remain alive in the ground.

Common broom is found over the greater part of Europe, but is local in Britain, being commonest on sandy soils in the east. It is tolerant of poor soil and grows especially on heaths and other sandy places. On railway embankments and other slopes it is planted or sown to prevent landslides. Broom is also frequently planted to provide food for game.

92. Gorse, Furze, Whin, *Ulex europaeus*

'Gorse' comes from Anglo-Saxon *gorst*, and 'furze' from Anglo-Saxon *fyrs*. The name 'whin', used mainly in Scotland, is of Norse derivation. In Welsh, gorse is called *eithin*. One Gaelic name is *droighneach*, thorny bush; another is *conusg*.

On this evergreen bush most of the

leaves, and the tips of the branches, have stiff, sharp thorns. Other leaves, which do not develop in that way, have three leaflets, but these appear only on quite young plants, or on very vigorous shoots.

The bush may be a little over 6 ft. high, but rarely grows taller. In Scotland, as also in Scandinavia, it suffers occasionally from frost in the winter, and is sometimes frosted down to the ground.

The bright yellow flowers have the typical pea-family form; the calyx is covered with persistent brown hairs, and the flowers have a strong musky odour. The short hairy pods are a dark greyish-blue in colour; they open in dry weather with a sharp crack, and the empty pods are twisted. Flowering begins in April and continues during two or three months, and there may again be many flowers in autumn.

Gorse is common on waste ground everywhere, but it will not grow on the poorest of soil.

European gorse is certainly a wild bush only in the British Isles and in the Iberian Peninsula, France and Belgium; but it is found over a large part of central Europe as an escape from cultivation. Two other species, namely western gorse, *Ulex gallii*, and dwarf gorse, *Ulex minor*, are distinguished by botanists on fine technical points; both form low compact bushes, sometimes only a foot high.

Holly Family, *Aquifoliaceae*.

93. Holly, *Ilex aquifolium*

'Holly' comes from the Anglo-Saxon *holen*, and is connected with Welsh *celyn* and Gaelic *cuillean*.

Holly is one of our very few wild evergreen broad-leaved trees. Under favourable conditions it may reach a height of 60 ft., but is usually a bush forming undergrowth.

The leaves are alternate, hard and leathery; the upper-surfaces are glossy and dark green, while the under-surfaces are dull and light green. On the lower part of the stem the leaves are waved, and bordered with strong prickly teeth, while higher up the stem they are often oval, thornless and rather narrower than the thorny leaves.

Flowering takes place in June. The inconspicuous white flowers grow in small clusters in the axils of the leaves. They are usually unisexual, and of the same sex on any one plant, so that individual trees may be either male or female. This explains why many garden holly bushes never bear berries.

The fruits, which are the size of peas, are four-seeded drupes. They are bright coral-red and remain on the trees into February. Birds, especially thrushes, eat these berries. At Christmas holly is much in demand for decorations.

Holly likes a mild winter climate; thus it is most vigorous in our western districts. It also grows wild in western and southern Europe, North Africa, parts of Asia Minor, the Caucasus and northern Asia.

The wood, which is whitish, hard and heavy, is used for turnery and inlay work.

Spindle Family, Celastraceae.

94. Spindle Tree,
Euonymus europaeus

The name of 'spindle tree' records the fact that the hard white wood of this bush was used for spindles before the spinning wheel was invented.

One Welsh name is *pisgwydd*, meaning bladder-tree, from the quaint fruits; another is *llwyn addurnol*, the decorative bush.

The spindle tree is usually a bush up to 15 ft. high, but sometimes it is a small tree and may occasionally reach a height of 25 ft.

The young branches are dark green, round or four-angled (almost square), and have four longitudinal stripes. The older branches are greyish-brown to reddish-brown, and often have an edging of cork.

The leaves are opposite, elliptical to lance-shaped, finely serrated and bluish-green on the under-sides. In autumn the leaves have a deep red colour.

The four-petalled flowers are greenish-yellow, small and rather inconspicuous; they unfold in May to June. Each flower has four sepals, four petals, four stamens, and a two-celled ovary. Nectar is contained in these flowers, and they are pollinated by the smaller insects. The fruit is a four-lobed pink, light red, or scarlet capsule which contains 2–4 seeds, each with an orange seed coat. When the capsule opens, the seeds are for a time suspended on a long seed-string.

The distinctive fruits and deep autumn colouring of the spindle tree fully justify its use as an ornamental shrub.

The white or pale yellow wood is finely porous and hard, and has no distinct heartwood. It is used for small turnery such as knitting needles, manicure sticks, pegs, etc.

Spindle is the only wild woody plant in northern Europe which contains guttapercha in the bark.

In Britain the spindle tree is very common on chalk, limestone, and lime-rich soils, but is unusual elsewhere. The total range of this species includes most of Europe and western Siberia, Asia Minor, the Caucasus and Turkestan.

Maple Family, Aceraceae.

Norway maple *Sycamore* *Field maple*

95. Norway Maple,
Acer platanoides

'Maple' comes from Anglo-Saxon *mapel* and Old Scots *mapulder*, both linked with Low German *Mapeldorn*. 'Norway' records the country from which it was introduced.

Both Norway maple and sycamore were formerly confused with plane (*Platanus*) on account of the similarity of their leaf forms, and because of the similar character of the barks of sycamore and plane. This former confusion of species is the origin of the Latin specific names *platanoides* and *pseudoplatanus* which mean, respectively, 'resembling plane' and 'false plane'.

Norway maple, sycamore and field maple have opposite, palmately-lobed leaves. The branching is monopodial, and the typical forked branches can be seen in the crowns of old maples and sycamores.

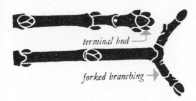

terminal bud

forked branching →

The flowers of these trees have five petals, which, like the sepals, are yellowish-green. Some of the flowers are hermaphrodite, with normally-developed stamens and styles. Some are female flowers with rudimentary stamens, and some are male flowers with rudimentary stigmas. These three types of flowers may be found on the same tree and even in the same inflorescence, but there are also wholly male and wholly female individuals.

The fruits of these three species are, when ripe, divided into two halves, each of which consists of a nut with a very large wing which has forked veins. These wings help the seed to be dispersed by the wind.

Norway maple grows up to 81 ft. tall. The young branches are greenish, later becoming brown, and finally grey. The winter buds are reddish, glabrous and contain milky juice, which is best seen when they are cut open with a sharp knife. The stems of young trees have smooth bark, but the bark cracks longitudinally with age and this produces regular furrows.

The leaves, which are about 6 in. wide, are five-lobed with broad incisions, the bays of which are usually round. The lobes are remotely and sharply toothed (acuminate). Both surfaces of the leaves are a fresh green colour. In autumn Norway maple has most attractive colours, with various shades of gold and yellow. In spring also, the young leaves show russet tints as they unfold. When trees stand in the shade, the leaves are so arranged in relation to each other that as much light as possible falls on their surfaces. This pattern of leaves is called a 'leaf mosaic'.

The bright yellowish-green flowers grow in upright inflorescences. As the flowers—and the leaves—unfold in the first weeks of May, and flowering is often very profuse, Norway maple at this time stands out from other trees.

The flowers contain nectar and are visited by many insects.

The wings of the fruits are almost horizontally extended from each other, and the part which contains the seeds is almost flat. The nut and wings are together $1\frac{1}{2}$–2 in. long.

The wood is yellowish-white to light reddish. It is very hard and has no distinct heartwood. It is used for joinery, furniture, and turnery.

In Britain, Norway maple is grown mainly for ornament, but a little has been planted for timber.

The natural distribution of Norway maple includes the greater part of Europe, except Britain and Holland, and extends into Armenia and the Caucasus.

96. Sycamore, *Acer pseudoplatanus*

'Sycamore' comes from the Latin *sycomorus*, meaning 'fig-mulberry', and arises from confusion with an eastern tree mentioned in the Bible.

Sycamore has also been called 'great maple'. In Scotland, the common name for both tree and timber is 'plane', arising from confusion with the true planes of the genus *Platanus*.

Sycamore reaches larger dimensions than Norway maple, both in height and circumference; the British records are 117 ft. tall and 19 ft. round. The greyish-brown branches produce large green buds, which are up to one-third of an inch long, and do not contain milky juice. The bark on the stems of older trees is light greyish-brown, and peels off in large irregular flakes.

The leaves are 3–6 in. wide, five-lobed, with narrow incisions which are pointed at the base. The lobes are coarsely serrated. The upper-sides of the leaves are dark green, and the under-sides are pale bluish-green or—in one common wood-land variety—more or less reddish.

The flowers unfold early in May, shortly after the leaves, and grow in long, green, hanging and compound racemes.

The wings of the fruit are at acute or right angles to each other. The seed-bearing parts are strongly domed.

The wood is white to yellowish, hard, and has a silky lustre. Sycamore has many uses including furniture, parquet blocks, various forms of joinery and turnery, and violin backs. As firewood it burns excellently, and faggots are another product of this tree. 'Bird's eye maple' is an especially valuable form of sycamore wood which is found from time to time. This and 'wavy' sycamore are used for decorative veneers.

Sycamore does not grow wild in Britain, but was introduced long ago and planted in parks and woodlands. As the seed is usually produced in large quantities and is very easily dispersed, sycamore has now gained a footing in nearly all our older woods, especially on humus-rich soils, where large groups of these trees are often found.

The natural range of sycamore is very difficult to define, as for hundreds of years the tree has been planted outside the area in which it was originally indigenous. This species is thought to be native in large areas of central Europe, especially the Pyrenees, the Alps and the Carpathians.

97. Field Maple, *Acer campestre*

This, our original and only native maple, is called 'field' (from the Latin specific name *campestre*) to distinguish it from the others. It is now mainly a hedgerow tree. For 'maple', see No. 95.

The Welsh name for field maple, now also applied to sycamore, is *masarn*. This is the root of the English 'mazer', a goblet, since field maple is the traditional timber for the old Welsh craft of bowl and spoon carving.

In contrast to Norway maple and sycamore, field maple is often merely a large bush, but occasionally it forms a tall tree up to 86 ft. high, and as much as 12 ft. round.

The young branches are at first green, but quickly become light reddish-brown, with light-brown longitudinal stripes. There are very often cork ribs on the branches. The bark of the stem is very light, corky, rugged, and irregularly netted.

The buds, including terminal ones, are small; in contrast to the previous *Acer* species, the bud scales have felted edges. Both the buds and the leaf stalks contain milky juice.

The leaves are smaller than those of the last species, only 2–4 in. wide, three- to five-lobed, with broadly incised, often entire lobes. The under-surfaces of the leaves have downy hair, at least along the veins.

The greenish flowers are in upright umbels, consisting of a few flowers which come out soon after leafing in May. The winged fruits are about 1 in. long, and in line with each other. The fruit-bearing part is flattened and rough. In autumn, field maple has bright yellow leaves.

The wood, which is of a slightly more reddish colour than that of sycamore, can be used for the same purposes; but owing to its small size, most goes for turnery.

Field maple is not used as a forest tree, but is sometimes planted in parks and gardens both as a free-standing ornamental tree, and for hedges. As a wild tree, it is most common in the south and east, especially on chalk and limestone soils. Field maple extends over most of Europe, south-west Russia, Algeria and Asia Minor.

Horse Chestnut Family, Hippocastanaceae.

98. Horse Chestnut,
Aesculus hippocastanum

The first part of the name 'horse chestnut' merely means that the fruits are unsuitable for human consumption, while the second part refers to their resemblance to the fruits of sweet chestnut. The name has nothing to do with the fact that horse chestnuts can be used for fodder. It is however true that the seeds have sometimes been used as a remedy for coughs in horses. The name 'conker', applied to the nut, is a corruption of 'conqueror'.

Horse chestnut may be a large tree up to 107 ft. high and 20 ft. round, with a beautiful arched crown. The branches of older trees have a typical curved form. The longitudinal growth of the branches is monopodial, that is to say each year it continues from the terminal bud unless this contains a flower. In that case the growth continues from lateral buds, and produces the typically forked branches, which characterize all older trees with opposite leaves.

The young branches are yellowish-brown to reddish-brown, and at first are brown-felted. The bark on the stem is smooth in youth, but peels off in thin flakes on older trees. The buds, especially the terminal buds, are large, brown and sticky.

The palmately compound leaves

have 5–7 leaflets with main stalks up to 8 in. long. When quite young they are strongly whitish-yellow-felted, and hang downwards in a distinctive way. The leaflets are sessile and doubly serrated. In autumn the leaves fall and leave large horseshoe-shaped scars on the branches. The leaves unfold at the beginning of May.

Flowering is usually profuse, and is an impressive sight in late May. The flowers are in cone-shaped panicles which are up to one foot long, and may almost cover the tree. Each flower has a calyx, consisting of five sepals, and an irregular corolla, consisting of 4–5 white petals. There is a yellow blotch, which later becomes red, at the base of each petal. There are from five to eight stamens, and a three-celled ovary.

The fruit is a more or less prickly capsule with three sections. Usually, in fact, it contains only one large, brown, smooth and shiny seed with a large round greyish spot. This spot is scarred by the seed's attachment to the seed base, and is called the 'navel'.

In addition to being a favourite —and cheap—toy for children, these 'chestnuts' (which have nothing to do with the edible sweet chestnuts) have several possible uses on account of their content of bitter tannin substances, saponin, etc. They were used in former times as a remedy for vomiting. In addition the seeds, when crushed and ground, but otherwise unprepared, have been used as a form of soap which dissolves fat and oils.

However, in practice, in Britain at least, horse chestnuts are never put to any practical use.

Horse chestnut is a valued tree in deer parks as the seeds provide excellent food for deer.

The wood is not particularly valuable. It is white, soft and easily cleft and has no distinct heartwood. It has been used for kitchen tables (the white scoured variety), hat blocks and fruit storage shelves. It is now used as firewood, and sometimes for boxes.

Horse chestnut has no particular value as a forest tree, and when it is planted in woodlands this is either for the sake of deer, or for aesthetic reasons. It is much used as an ornamental tree although it is unsuitable for small gardens as it casts too much shade, and because it becomes very large.

The original home of horse chestnut is Asia Minor, northern Greece, and Albania, but it has been widely planted elsewhere.

Buckthorn Family, Rhamnaceae.

99. Alder Buckthorn,
Frangula alnus

Called 'alder' because it grows in the same marshy places as the alder tree, and 'buckthorn' because it resembles purging buckthorn, to which it is closely related. It has, however, no thorns at all. In some districts it is mistakenly called 'dogwood'. (See No. 109.)

Alder buckthorn is a small bush, which only occasionally reaches a height of 15–20 ft. The branching habit is very open, and the slender branches spread out almost horizontally. In this species there is no division into long and short shoots —there are only long shoots. The bark is greyish-brown and covered with many long and light-coloured lenticels. The buds are bare— i.e. there are no actual bud scales— and brown-felted.

The leaves are alternate, entire, and glabrous, and have 7–9 pairs of lateral veins.

The flowers, which come out from June onwards during the summer, have five petals and are hermaphrodite (having both sexes present). They are whitish-green, small and inconspicuous, and form small inflorescences in the leaf axils.

The fruits are three-seeded drupes which are first green, then red, and when fully ripe, black. They are dispersed by birds.

The wood has a narrow yellow sapwood and reddish-yellow heartwood. It was used as late as 1946 as charcoal in the manufacture of high quality gunpowder, particularly for time fuses where even burning is essential.

A mild laxative, buckthorn bark, is made from the dried bark. The fruit and bark when fresh have an emetic effect.

Alder buckthorn is common on acid and poor soils, and grows in scrub and as underwood in woodlands where there is sufficient light. It is also found, again on acid ground, in association with willows near lakes and bogs.

The range of this species covers the British Isles and almost the whole of Europe, including Scandinavia, the Caucasus and Asia Minor.

100. Purging Buckthorn,
Rhamnus cathartica

'Purging' refers to the powerful purgative properties of the berries, which are still used in herbal medicine. This bush is closely related to *Rhamnus purshiana*, the Californian shrub that yields cascara.

The Danish name *Korsved*, cross wood, refers to the cross-branching due to the opposite shoots. This name was inspired by the Passion story of the New Testament, and the thorns of this tree have been thought of in connection with Our Lord's crown of thorns. Because of the cross formed by the branches, and on account of the thorns, this plant was used as a protection against witchcraft and magic.

Purging buckthorn is usually larger than alder buckthorn and is more often a tree in form, reaching heights up to 30 ft. It has quite a different form of branching, as there are both short shoots (dwarf shoots) and long shoots. When the tip of the long shoot dies, it remains on the tree and becomes a spine, after which the longitudinal growth continues from the foremost buds. The bark on older branches and stems is nearly black.

In contrast to the last species, purging buckthorn has distinct bud scales. They are brownish-violet and have frayed margins.

The leaves are opposite, but not in the exact sense. They are 1½–3 in.

long and are broadly ovate with serrated margins. The three or sometimes five pairs of veins are curved, and the apex of the leaf is often twisted.

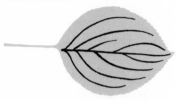

Flowering takes place in June, with small inconspicuous sweet-scented flowers, which have four petals and are unisexual. Purging buckthorn usually has only male flowers or only female flowers, i.e. it is dioecious.

The fruits are drupes. They are the size of peas, black when ripe, and normally contain four seeds. In autumn, after leaf-fall, some of the female plants may be completely covered with fruits, and are most decorative.

The wood has light-yellow sapwood and reddish-brown heartwood. It is hard and dense, and in section shows a flame structure. There are no special uses for it.

Purging buckthorn is less common than alder buckthorn, and grows especially on the edges of woodlands and in scrub, thickets and hedgerows. It is only common on the chalk formations of the south and east, where it thrives on the very poorest and driest of soils.

It is a host plant for 'crown rust', a parasitic fungus which attacks oats, etc. This is shown on the leaves of purging buckthorn by orange-coloured specks, deepening into spots.

Purging buckthorn is found wild, though only locally, over most of Britain, and nearly all Europe.

Lime Family, Tiliaceae.

101. Small-Leaved Lime,
Tilia cordata

The name 'lime' occurs throughout north-west Europe as *Linde* in German and Dutch, 'linden' (-tree) in English, and *lind* in Swedish and old Norse. It is apparently connected with the Swedish *linda*, to bind or wrap round, and with the German *Lind*, which means the bast of lime. Thus it seems to refer to the bast which has been obtained from the bark since very early times. The tree is also called in English and German 'bast', in Anglo-Saxon *baste-tree*, and in Swedish *bast(e)träd*. In addition, the Latin name *Tilia* is connected with the Latin *tela*, something woven. The Welsh names for lime tree are *palalwyf*, stout-boled elm, and *llwyf teil*, lime-elm; the Gaelic name is *teile*.

In winter these trees can be easily recognized by the sharply-defined outline of their crowns. In summer they are thickly leaved and cast much shade. Limes are often large trees with heights up to 150 ft.

The formation of the shoots is sympodial.

The buds of lime are ovate, with only 2–3 outer bud scales, of which the outermost is particularly large. Like the branches, the buds are reddish on the side facing the light.

The leaves are arranged alternately and in two rows (distichous), with long stalks. They are more or less heart-shaped, often obliquely so, with serrated edges. In the angles between the midrib and the lateral veins, on the under-side of the leaf, there are small tufts of short and close-set hairs.

The seedlings of lime are characteristic with their palmately lobed

leaves; often they do not spring up until the seeds have lain for eighteen months in the ground.

The five-petalled hermaphrodite flowers are whitish-yellow, scented and rich in nectar. They grow placed on a long-stalked inflorescence (cyme), with a wing-like leaf at the base, which enables the seeds to be dispersed by wind. The fruits are nuts with 1–2 seeds.

Small-leaved lime is usually the smallest of the three lime species (although it may grow as tall as 105 ft.), and has the smallest leaves. They are frequently glabrous, except for the hairs in the angles between the veins, green on the upper-sides and usually clearly bluish-green on the under-sides. The young shoots are glabrous, or have a few adjacent hairs. The bark of the stem is thin, brownish and smooth in youth; later it becomes longitudinally furrowed and very dark.

The leaves unfold at the end of April and flowering takes place in June. It is one of the few forest trees to be pollinated by insects. In most other forest trees the pollen is dispersed by wind.

The fruits of small-leaved lime are thin-shelled, round and have five indistinct ribs.

The wood when freshly cut is white, but often becomes rather reddish when dried. It is light and soft and warps very little. There is no distinct heartwood. It is used for fine carving, turnery, musical instruments, piano keys, hat blocks, and, on account of its stability, for artificial limbs. The wonderful wood carvings of Grinling Gibbons were always done in lime. Lime is the best wood for making artists' charcoal.

The bark contains so much bast that at one time it was in great demand as a binding material for garden and other purposes. The dried flowers have been, and are still to some extent, used for lime tea.

Lime honey is known for its aromatic taste. The sweet sticky coating known as 'honey-dew', which often appears in summer on the leaves of lime, has nothing to do with true lime honey. It is the sugar-containing excreta from a leaf aphid, which in large numbers seeks out limes. Various insects, including bees, collect this excreta, which may reduce the quality of the bees' honey.

Small-leaved lime grows wild in many parts of England and Wales, but is not at all common. It is rarely planted as a forest tree and is therefore found mainly in natural woodland. This species may be seen here and there in parks, especially as an avenue tree. The general range includes Scandinavia

and the greater part of Europe, especially the eastern regions.

102. Large-Leaved Lime,
Tilia platyphyllos

For the name-derivation, see No. 101.

Large-leaved lime generally becomes a larger tree than small-leaved lime and similarly the annual shoots, buds and leaves are normally larger. The leaves are almost equally green on both sides. In contradistinction to small-leaved lime, the leaves, annual shoots and buds are distinctly downy.

Leafing and flowering take place rather earlier than in the small-leaved lime. The flowers grow in cymes consisting of 3–4 blooms. The fruits have thick shells and are hard. When ripe they have five clearly-projecting ribs. The seeds have a fair germination percentage.

Large-leaved lime, during the favourable climate of the post-glacial warm period, grew wild over the greater part of northern Europe. There are now only one or two places in Britain where it can be found as a wild tree, notably the Severn and Wye Valleys. The main area of natural distribution of this lime is central and southern Europe.

103. Common Lime,
Tilia vulgaris

For the name-derivation, see No. 101.

The third of our limes, common lime, appears to be a spontaneous hybrid, which has arisen many times, between small-leaved lime and large-leaved lime. It resembles small-leaved lime, but the under-sides of the leaves are pure green. The leaves and shoots are glabrous. The flowers grow in cymes of 7–11 blooms, and the fruits have thick shells with indistinct ribs.

Common lime is the most frequently planted species in avenues and on road sides, and reaches 152 ft. tall. Although it is sometimes regarded as sterile, its seeds may in fact germinate eighteen months after they fall.

Tamarisk Family,
Tamaricaceae.

104. Myricaria, *Myricaria germanica*

The name 'Myricaria', used as the Latin generic name, and as both English and Danish common names, was coined by the Swedish botanist Linnaeus from the Greek root *myrica*, which means a tamarisk. Myricaria is nearly related to, and closely resembles, the true tamarisk of the Bible.

This species is a twiggy bush not more than 6 ft. high. It has yellowish-green or shiny reddish-brown shoots, and small greyish-green leaves which grow on the numerous short shoots that arise along the long annual shoots. The short shoots die off in the autumn.

The small light-red flowers grow

partly at the tips of the annual shoots in July to August, and partly on the sparsely-leaved short shoots in June. The flower-bearing short shoots also die in the autumn.

The natural habitat of this plant is on damp stony gravels or sandy soil. In England it occurs only as a cultivated plant. It is distributed throughout the mountainous regions of Europe and western Asia.

Daphne Family, *Thymelaeaceae*.

105. Daphne, *Daphne mezereum*

'Daphne' is a Greek name which was originally applied to the sweet bay tree, *Laurus nobilis*.

Daphne is a bush up to 3 ft. high, with twig-like branches. The branches are light greyish-brown, and the bark, especially when green, has a very strong smell.

The leaves are alternate, entire, glabrous and lance-shaped. They are about 3 in. long and 1 in. wide. The upper-surfaces of the leaves are fresh green, and the under-surfaces bluish-green. The hermaphrodite flowers, which each have a fourfold perianth, come from flower buds which are usually in twos, one above the other, in the leaf axils. There are no petals, but the sepals and flower receptacle have a beautiful bright mauve, or sometimes a white, colour. The time of flowering largely depends on the climate during the winter, and may begin as early as December in mild years. In more severe winters the flowers are later, and may even be as late as March. The flowers, which may completely cover the branches of the bush, have a strong, almost stupefying smell. They are pollinated by bees.

The fruits are scarlet berries. They are very decorative, but extremely poisonous. Ten to twelve berries would be fatal to an adult person. However, these berries have such a sharp and burning taste that one would not voluntarily eat them. In addition, other parts of the plant are poisonous and there have been cases of horses and goats etc. being poisoned.

A yellow dye can be obtained from the bark, and a beautiful red colour, used by painters, from the berries.

As a wild plant daphne is rare in Britain, but it does occur as a true native on limestone formations in northern England, such as the Furness Fells. It is very commonly cultivated as a delightful garden shrub.

The natural range of daphne includes Europe, Siberia, the Caucasus, and Asia Minor. Daphne prefers damp soils rich in humus and nutrients, and often occurs in mixed beech forests in mountainous regions.

105a. Spurge Laurel, *Daphne laureola*

Called 'spurge' from a fancied resemblance to the true spurges of the genus *Euphorbia*, and 'laurel' because of slight resemblance to the sweet bay tree, *Laurus nobilis*.

The spurge laurel (not illustrated) is an uncommon undershrub, only a foot or two high, which grows mainly in beechwoods on chalk or limestone soils in the south and east. It has dark green, oval, leathery, evergreen leaves. Its fragrant flowers, borne in clusters along the stem in March or April, are green and inconspicuous; they are succeeded by black berries.

Elaeagnus Family, Eleagnaceae.

106. Sea Buckthorn,
Hippophaë rhamnoides

Called 'sea' from its usual seashore home, and 'buckthorn' from its resemblance to purging buckthorn (No. 100).

This unusual and distinctive plant is usually a bush up to 10 ft. high, or occasionally a tree up to 20 ft. tall, thickly branched and bearing many spines. The leaves are narrow, linear and greyish-green on the upper-surfaces; the under-surfaces and the young shoots are silvery, and covered with shield-shaped hairs.

Suckers

The flowers, which unfold slightly before or at the same time as the leaves in May to June, are quite inconspicuous, but the flowering is notable in that sea buckthorn is dioecious. In winter the difference in sex can clearly be seen on the older plants, as the flower buds of the male plant are large, while those of the female plant are small.

The decorative berry-like fruits —which in fact are nuts surrounded by a juicy fruit base—appear in large quantities, and in various colours from pale yellow to bright orange. They have an exceptionally high content of vitamin C, and can be used for making marmalade. They are eaten by birds, especially poultry.

Sea buckthorn produces suckers in large numbers, especially on hills or slopes. They appear in the spring and it is reported that a single plant can, in the course of five years, produce 10–20 new bushes within a space of from 1–3 ft. On the whole the root-forming ability is great, and even old branches are able to strike root.

This plant is also able to establish itself on drifting sand, and has therefore been used for the fixation of dunes.

The roots are distinctive in that they have small nodules which enable the tree to utilize the free nitrogen in the air, and on poor soils this is of great value to the plant.

Sea buckthorn is an extremely light-demanding plant, and the seedlings are unable to grow in the shade of the parent bush. Another feature is that both the lowest and the innermost branches of the bush quickly die as a result of the shade from the upper and outside branches.

This need for light determines the geographical distribution of this bush. It seems likely that it was formerly far more widely dispersed than at present, but that in the course of time it has been supplanted by more shade-bearing trees and bushes. Therefore sea buckthorn now grows only where there is little competition from other bushes, i.e. in certain mountainous districts, along rivers, and at the coast.

The focal point of the range of sea buckthorn lies in central, west, and east Asia, but this plant also appears on a small scale over the greater part of Europe. It is truly native, though rare, in Britain, being found wild only at scattered points on the east coast of Scotland and England.

Ivy Family, Hederaceae.

107. Ivy, *Hedera helix*

The name 'ivy' comes from Anglo-Saxon *ifig*, and is related to the German *Efeu*, signifying bitter, from the taste of the berries.

In Welsh, ivy is *eiddew* or *iorwg;* in Gaelic *eidheam.*

Ivy is a climbing woody plant, or a liana, which, by means of clinging roots on the inner or under-side of the stem, is able to climb high into trees or up hillsides or walls. It climbs best on rough-barked trees such as elm and ash, and less easily on smooth-barked trees, e.g. beech.

It is not essential for the plant to climb, as it can live on the forest floor, where it often forms an extensive green carpet. However, ivy only flowers when it comes up into the light, either at the top of a tree or on a rock face or wall.

The leaf shoots and the flower shoots differ considerably. On the leaf shoots, which creep along the ground or climb upwards, the leaves are arranged in two rows and are palmately veined and palmately lobed. The veins often appear whitish on the background of the shiny dark green upper leaf-surface.

On the flowering shoots the leaves are placed on all sides, and are pinnately veined, oval and entire. The white colouring is usually absent from the veins, and therefore the leaves seem a darker green. The flowering shoots are branched on all sides, and do not bear any clinging roots. Cuttings of these shoots develop into small bushes which do not themselves form clinging roots. These bushes are called *arborea* or 'tree' forms of ivy.

Flowering begins in September to October. Flowers are small and yellowish-green with five sepals, five petals, five stamens, and a five-celled ovary. They grow in a round inflorescence. The flowering is often so profuse that the whole of the flowering part of the plant is covered with blooms. The smell of the flowers, which is unpleasant to us, and the abundant nectar, attract many insects, especially flies and hornets.

In our climate the fruits, or berries, remain green all the winter and ripen the following year in May to June. When ripe they are bluish-black. The seeds have a high germination percentage, but only sprout when they are released from the flesh of the fruit, which contains substances which hinder germination.

Ivy, like holly, likes mild winters and relatively high air humidity. In severe winters the flowering shoots are sometimes killed by frost.

As a wild plant ivy is found throughout the British Isles and in western, central and southern Europe. In addition it grows in Asia Minor, northern Persia, Kurdestan and Lebanon, but is absent from the greater part of Russia.

Heath Family, *Ericaceae.*

108. Wild Rosemary,
Ledum palustre

So called from its resemblance to garden 'rosemary', *Rosmarinus officinalis*. This word is a compound of Latin *ros* and *marinus*, and means 'dew of the sea'.

Wild rosemary is an evergreen bush up to 3 ft. high. The narrow alternate leaves are leathery and have recurved margins. The under-sides of the leaves are covered with brownish-red down (felt).

The white flowers grow at the ends of the shoots, in half-umbellate inflorescences. They have a very strong aromatic smell which is rather like that of sweet gale. Both these plants have been used for flavouring beer, instead of hops.

The natural habitat of wild rosemary is in forest bogs where it may form large groups. It does not grow in Denmark, but is found in the eastern parts of Scandinavia and extends from there into Russia. It has been introduced to Scotland and grows wild in peaty boglands to the west of Stirling.

Dogwood Family, *Cornaceae.*

109. Dogwood, *Cornus sanguinea*

The name 'dogwood' was originally 'dagwood', and refers to the use of this bush's hard horny wood for 'dags' or skewers (cf. the word 'dagger').

This bush may be up to 12 ft. high and has long branches, which are reddish, particularly during winter. The reddish tinge occurs especially on the side of the branch which

faces the light. The buds are small and have no actual bud scales, but are surrounded by one or two pairs of small hairy leaves.

The leaves are opposite; they are ovate, entire and, like purging buckthorn, have 3–5 pairs of lateral veins which curve forwards each side of the midrib. In autumn the leaves turn a handsome deep red colour.

Flowering takes place in June–July and the white four-petalled flowers, which also have four sepals and 4–5 stamens, grow in striking half-umbellate inflorescences. They have a rather unpleasant smell, which is, however, attractive to various small insects.

The fruits, which are the size of peas, are black two-stoned drupes.

The wood is very hard and can be used for various forms of turnery work, though it is only available in small sizes.

Dogwood grows by preference on ground which is rich in nutrients, such as humus-rich calcareous soils. It is common in hedges, woodland fringes and forest scrub. In these places it often forms small thickets by means of root suckers. Very common on the chalk downs of southern England, it is the first bush to colonize abandoned pastures, to which its seeds are carried by the birds.

The general range of dogwood includes most of Europe, but with an eastern boundary from the Baltic to the Caspian Sea.

Olive Family, Oleaceae.

110. Ash, *Fraxinus excelsior*

The English name 'ash' comes from Anglo-Saxon *aesc* and also from the Danish *Ask*, which is a very old name in north-west Europe, though its ultimate origin and derivation are uncertain. It is known from the old Norse *askr* of the middle (Norse) period, and is common in English place-names dating from pre-Norman times. The Gaelic name is *uinnse*, and the Welsh is *onn*.

Ash is a forest tree which, under favourable conditions, may reach a height of 148 ft., and a girth of 19 ft. It often has a long clean stem with a particularly open arched crown.

The young branches are glabrous, light grey to olive green, and somewhat flattened at the ends. The buds are opposite, black and cork-felted.

The bark of the stem is light grey to olive green for a number of years; indeed the longer it remains so, the more the tree flourishes. Later it develops a typical rugged bark with close deep furrows.

The root system of ash largely consists of very strong flat spreading roots. The young roots can be recognized by their yellowish-white colour.

The leaves are opposite and pinnately compound, having many pairs of side leaflets and a single terminal one. Thus they may be composed of from 9–15 unstalked leaflets, which have serrated edges. When the leaves fall at the end of October, the leaflets often fall first, while the leaf stalk and main axis remain on the tree for some time. Leafing is late; normally ash is not fully in leaf until late May, when other trees and bushes—but not in some years the oak—are completely green.

The flowers unfold before the leaves. They grow in very compact inflorescences which are produced from lateral buds on short shoots of the previous year. There are hermaphrodite flowers, male flowers and female flowers. All these may be found on the same individual, but there are also purely male and purely female trees, and trees which bear hermaphrodite flowers *plus* either male or female flowers. Both sepals and petals are indistinct; male flowers have two stamens, and female flowers a two-celled ovary.

The fruits or 'keys' are winged nuts which remain on the tree for a long time, and are dispersed in the winter. If they are sown green they germinate at once, but otherwise they lie dormant in the soil for eighteen months. Foresters usually store them in sand pits for that period.

If it is to grow well, ash requires a very moist soil rich in humus and nutrients, but it will not tolerate stagnant water. These requirements mean that ash can seldom be grown over a large area, but is a species suitable for small plots. As the crown of this tree is light and therefore casts very little shade, there is often an underwood in an ash stand, composed of various bushes. In addition there is a rich herb and grass vegetation, consisting mainly of nitrogen-loving species.

The light-coloured sapwood of

ash is very narrow and consists of few annual rings. The heartwood has the same colour.

Ash wood is hard and elastic, and is one of the most valuable timbers produced in our forests. It is especially suitable for axe shafts and tool handles, for carts, agricultural implements, oars and skis. It is used for cooperage and furniture, and in the framing of cars, vans and buses.

In former times the use of ash leaves as winter fodder for cattle was very important in Scandinavia. As a result of this use, which extended to southern Europe, this species was spread by man and it is difficult to define its original range. Ash is regarded as wild over the greater part of Europe and the countries of the Caucasus. In Scotland it extends right to the far north-west of Sutherland and flourishes at Laxford Bridge near Cape Wrath.

111. Lilac, *Syringa vulgaris*

'Lilac' is derived from the Persian name *lilas;* this also means 'bluish', and refers to the colour of the flowers. The Welsh name is *lelog.*

The Latin name of *syringa* refers to the fact that flutes and other reed or pipe-shaped instruments or tools may be made from the slender branches, as the pith can be easily removed. The Greek word *syrinx,* from which the plant's Latin name *Syringa* is derived, actually means 'reed' or 'flute'.

Lilac is a tall bush, or a small tree, with smooth greyish branches and a rough (scabrous) stem bark, which peels off in thin flakes. The buds are ovoid and green, and on vigorous shoots they are often $\frac{1}{4}$ in. long.

The leaves are opposite, entire, ovate-cordate, and do not change colour before falling in autumn. The flowers are light violet or white, with petals united in a tube. They grow in terminal panicles and open in May to early June. The fruits are capsules with narrow winged seeds.

seed with seed-wing

Lilac is often planted in garden hedges and spreads by means of suckers. The many types of lilacs grown in gardens are hybrids of this common lilac.

Lilac appears to be wild in Hungary, Transylvania, Serbia and Asia Minor. However, it has been cultivated as an ornamental shrub since the Middle Ages, and grows in many places as an escape from cultivation.

The wood of lilac is heavy and hard, with light sapwood and light brown or purplish heartwood. It is used for high quality inlay work.

112. Privet, *Ligustrum vulgare*

'Privet' is an old word related to 'private', and arises from the use of this evergreen shrub for enclosed or 'privy' gardens.

The Danish name *Liguster* is a version of the Latin name of the plant, which is of classical origin and is used by many Roman writers. It is related to the verb *ligo*, to bind, since the supple twigs of the wild bush can be used for tying bundles.

This common plant may be a bush up to 10 ft. high. It has opposite, lance-shaped and entire leaves,

which are shiny dark green on the upper-surfaces and light green on the under-surfaces. In autumn they turn a violet colour, and by winter most have fallen. The young branches are glabrous and olive green; later they become grey.

The flowers, which have four petals, are white and funnel-shaped, and have an exceedingly sweet scent. They grow in compact panicles. The fruits are black berries and are used for decorative purposes.

In its natural habitat privet often forms thickets by means of suckers and layering. It is a common wild shrub in the south of England, and is specially frequent on the chalk. The general range of this species includes Europe as far as east Prussia, Poland and the southern Ukraine. In addition it is found in North Africa and western Asia.

The privet now so commonly grown as a garden hedge is not this native species, but the more closely-leaved, and truly evergreen, Japanese privet, *Ligustrum ovalifolium*. Privet is one of the most common hedge plants as it will stand heavy and frequent clipping.

Potato Family, Solanaceae.

113. Tea Tree, *Lycium halimifolium*

The full name of this attractive shrub is 'The Duke of Argyll's Tea Tree'. A certain Duke of Argyll was sent a specimen of this shrub, and also one of a real tea bush. The labels became mixed, and the Duke fondly grew the *Lycium* as a tea tree. It is also called 'box-thorn'.

Tea tree is a bush up to 10 ft. tall; the light grey branches are long, thin and curved, and some have spines. The leaves are lance-shaped, greyish-green and arranged spirally. The buds are very small and are often borne in small groups immediately above the leaf scar.

The long-stalked violet flowers grow singly, or occasionally 2–3 together, in the leaf axils. Flowering takes place from May and continues through the summer. The fruits are oblong scarlet berries.

As the tea tree is a tolerant and windfirm plant which will also stand salt spray, it is much planted for hedges on sandy soil near the sea; it is also naturalized along railway banks inland.

This species has a marked tendency to produce suckers and it is very easy to grow from cuttings.

Tea tree does not grow wild in Britain or Scandinavia, but is native in southern and central Europe, North Africa and western Asia.

Honeysuckle Family,
Caprifoliaceae.

114. Red-berried Elder,
Sambucus racemosa

'Red-berried' is self-explanatory; for 'elder' see No. 115.

Red-berried elder is a smaller bush than common elder (No. 115), with dark brown bark and lighter greyish branches, which have a large light-brown pith.

The buds are enclosed, ovoid to round, and have short stalks. The opposite, pinnately compound leaves are composed of 5–7 elliptical and serrated leaflets.

Flowering is in April to May, and the greenish-yellow flowers, with a rather mealy scent, grow in inflorescences resembling clusters of grapes. The fruits, which ripen in July, are an intense coral-red and very decorative. They are eaten and dispersed by birds.

In Scotland, and also throughout Denmark, the red-berried elder is fairly common in forests, woodland fringes and hedges where it now grows wild, having escaped from cultivation; but it is seldom seen in England. It was originally native in central and southern Europe and in northern Asia.

115. Common Elder,
Sambucus nigra

The name 'elder' comes from Anglo-Saxon *ellaern*, and is probably related to 'hollow', from the hollow character of the tree's smaller stems. The Scots name 'bore-tree' conveys the same idea.

The Welsh name, *ysgaw*, is probably derived from *cau*, meaning 'hollow', cf. *cawn* for (hollow) reeds. The Gaelic names, of uncertain origin, are *ruis* and *truim*.

Common elder is usually a bush composed of many stems and up to 15 ft. high, but sometimes it has the form of a tree, up to 40 ft. high and 7 ft. round. The annual shoots are green and have many prominent grey lenticels. Later the branches become grey and eventually have a deeply furrowed light-brown to grey, rugged bark. The vigorous young shoots appear almost herbaceous, and contain a thick white pith. Sometimes these shoots are killed by frost in winter, but normally they survive and develop into permanent stems.

The winter buds have 2–4 bud scales which do not completely close over the leaf blades, so that the latter are often visible. The terminal buds of the shoots often die, and as the inflorescences are situated at the extremities of the annual shoots, forked branching is common.

The leaves are opposite, and pinnately compound, with 5–7 elliptical and serrated leaflets. Leafing takes place very early, and in mild years may even begin before mid-winter.

Flowering takes place in June and is often very profuse. The flowers are small, yellowish-white, strongly scented and in five-branched umbels. Each has five sepals, five petals united in a tube, five stamens, and a three-celled ovary. The fruits, 'elderberries', are three-seeded drupes. When ripe they are blackish-violet and contain blackish-red juice. Many birds eat these berries and in consequence the seeds are widely dispersed in droppings.

The yellowish-white wood is heavy, hard and strong. It has no distinct heartwood. Elder wood is regarded as the best material for making wooden spoons.

This species prefers rich nitrogenous soils and often forms scrub or underwood in light forest stands.

Elder tea, made from the flowers, has a sudorific effect and is considered to be an effective remedy for the common cold. Syrup, pies, and wine can be made from the berries; they can also be eaten raw but their taste is insipid.

The green parts of the plant—the young bark, the leaves and the unripe fruits—contain a glucoside separated from prussic acid, and are therefore poisonous.

Common elder is regarded as being wild throughout Britain, most of Europe, the Caucasus, Asia Minor, Armenia and western Siberia.

116. Guelder Rose,
Viburnum opulus

This wild, native bush draws its name from a cultivated form, the 'guelder rose' that originated in the Dutch province of Guelderland. It is not, of course, a rose at all. Its other common name is 'snowball tree', from the shape and colour of its flower cluster.

This bush may be up to 15 ft. high. The annual shoots are light brown, while the older branches and stems have a greyish-yellow bark. The buds are reddish-brown, short-stalked, and provided with two pairs of bud scales, of which the outside pair is grown together so that there appears to be only one bud scale.

There is often forked branching either because the terminal buds die, or because instead of leaves they develop into an inflorescence.

The leaves are opposite, three- to five-lobed, and toothed. The leaf stalk has distinct greenish glands. In autumn the leaves turn a beautiful yellow, or red to reddish-brown.

The flowers, which unfold in June, grow in large flat inflorescences (umbellate clusters). The outer flowers, which are sterile and merely serve to attract the pollinating insects, have large wheel-shaped corollas and are pure white. The inner flowers, which alone contain the nectar, are bisexual, small and yellowish-white, with bell-shaped corollas. The fruits are red drupes with a single seed. Like the leaves and bark, the fruits are poisonous to us, although not to the birds.

A variety of guelder rose, called Snowball, is much grown in gardens; it bears very large white and sterile flowers in conical inflorescences. Because it is sterile, and does not grow from branch cuttings it is increased by layering.

Guelder rose requires moist nutritious soil and is often found as undergrowth in alder woods; it also grows in hedges. The roots sometimes form suckers.

This species grows wild, not only in Britain and the Scandinavian countries, but throughout the greater part of Europe and in western and northern Asia.

116a. Wayfaring Tree,
Viburnum lantana

The attractive name of 'wayfaring tree', or 'wayfarer', was coined by the herbalist Gerard in 1597, because he encountered this tree so often along the hedges beside the drove-roads over the chalk downs between Wessex and London. Its original name was 'hoar withy'—'hoar' from its downy white leaves, and 'withy' from the pliancy of its twigs.

This small tree (not illustrated) may readily be identified by its opposite, oval leaves, with finely toothed margins, which are clad in a white woolly covering of fine hairs. This downy covering, which extends over twigs and buds also, helps to restrict the loss of moisture through transpiration; for the wayfarer flourishes on the very dry soils of the chalk. Its buds are 'naked', bearing no scales over the young leaves, and each bud has a distinct stalk. The twigs are exceptionally tough and flexible— easily bent but hard to break.

Wayfarer bears umbels of white flowers in June; each flower has five green sepals, five white petals, five stamens, and a three-celled ovary. Its berries ripen through green, yellow, and scarlet to black. They have a sour smell that attracts only the birds. Wayfarer is only common in the south-east, where it often spreads over deserted downland pastures. It rarely grows more than 20 ft. in height.

117. Snowberry,
Symphoricarpus racemosus (S. albus)

The name refers to the snow-white fruits.

Snowberry is a bush 3–5 ft. high with thin, strongly branched shoots. The leaves are small, oval to egg-shaped and often simple, but sometimes lobed.

The small light-red flowers unfold in May and flowering continues until October. The berries are white, partially filled with air, and about ½ in. in diameter. They remain on the bush until far into the winter.

Snowberry grows wild in North America. However, it is commonly planted in gardens and hedges and from these sources has spread into our woods.

118. Honeysuckle,
Lonicera periclymenum

The name 'honeysuckle' comes from Anglo-Saxon *hunnisucce*, and arises from the fact that one can suck honey—or at least nectar—from the end of the flower. Another name is 'woodbine' from the growth of the stem as a 'bine' or twiner.

In Welsh, honeysuckle is called *gwyddfid*, from *gwydd*, a wood, and *bid*, a hedge, possibly because it binds trees together in a thicket. Another Welsh name is *melys y pia*, the honey of the magpie.

An expressive Gaelic name is *lus a' chraois*, herb of the wide mouth, from the gaping corolla; another Gaelic name is *iadhshlat*.

Wild honeysuckle is a liana which entwines and climbs trees and bushes. It climbs to a considerable height and can be so strong that the plant which is entwined becomes distorted. Hence it has to be cut out as a weed in forest plantations.

The buds are long and slender, and often so far open, even in winter, that at least the tip of the green leaf can be seen; the leaves unfold as early as April. The branches, except for the youngest, have hollow pith.

The leaves are opposite, elliptical and normally entire. The upper-surfaces are dark green, and the lower-surfaces are blue-green.

The inflorescences are at the extremities of the shoots. The flower is irregular and funnel-shaped, with a narrow corolla tube one inch long. On the outside the flowers are reddish, and inside they are light yellow, but the colour varies considerably. In daytime the scent of the flowers is not particularly strong, but in the evening it is very strong and aromatic. As the nectar is situated at the bottom of the long corolla tube, it can only be reached by insects with a long proboscis, and among these are the hawk moths of the Sphingidae group (e.g. the privet hawk moth). Flowering takes place in June to July, but quite often there is also a sparse flowering in the autumn. The fruits are dark red berries with a few seeds.

Wild honeysuckle is not exacting as regards soil, but is found in light woodlands and scrub on extremely varying soils. It grows wild throughout Britain, in Scandinavia and in most of Europe, but not further east than Germany and Italy. In addition this plant is found in the Caucasus and Asia Minor.

119. Blue-Berried Honeysuckle,
Lonicera coerulea

The English name is self-explanatory. The Latin, *Lonicera*, is taken from the name of a German botanist, Adam Lonitzer.

This strongly-branched bush reaches a height up to 5 ft. The branches are yellow to reddish-brown, with easily peeling bark and no hollow pith. The annual shoots are often glaucous. The pointed buds are set almost at right-angles to the branches, and are in groups of 2–4, arranged immediately above each other.

The leaves, which are oval and short-stalked, are downy when young. On vigorous shoots the bases of the leaf-stalks of the opposite leaves are grown together, and surround the branch like a collar.

The small yellowish-white flowers grow in pairs in the leaf axils on a short common stalk. Flowering is in May. The fruits are globular and over $\frac{1}{2}$ in. in diameter. They are black, with a coating of bluish wax.

Blue-berried honeysuckle grows best on non-calcareous soils. It is uncommon as a wild plant, but occurs in Scotland, Sweden, Norway and Finland, the Pyrenees, the Carpathians, the Balkans, the Caucasus and northern and central Russia. In addition this species is found in northern Asia, Japan and North America.

120. Woody Honeysuckle,
Lonicera xylosteum

Called 'woody' honeysuckle from the texture of its stem; also known as 'fly' honeysuckle. The Latin specific name, *xylosteum*, refers to the hardness of the wood.

Woody honeysuckle is a bush up to 10 ft. high, which is often fully branched from the ground. The hollow branches are light grey, and downy, with pointed enclosed buds which do not show green like those of common honeysuckle. Branches lying on the ground easily take root. The leaves are downy, oval to elliptical, entire and short-stalked.

The flowers, which are small and whitish-yellow, grow in pairs on a common stalk $\frac{1}{2}$ in. long. Flowering is in May to June. The bright red berries are formed in pairs which often grow together at the base.

Woody honeysuckle grows as woodland undergrowth on good soils and is rather rare in Britain. It grows throughout most of Europe and in the Caucasus and Siberia.

Box Family, Buxaceae

121. Box, *Buxus sempervirens*

'Box' comes from Anglo-Saxon *bocs* and is related to German *Buchs*.

Box is a small evergreen tree, seldom over 10 ft. high, found wild on Box Hill in Surrey and at a few other places on chalk and limestone in the south. It is readily known by its small, opposite, oval, leathery leaves, which are dark green above and pale green below. Its tiny inconspicuous flowers are greenish-white in colour, and appear in leaf axils in May. The male flowers have four sepals and four stamens; the female flowers, which arise nearer the tips of the same twigs, have four sepals and a three-styled ovary. The fruit is a greenish-white papery capsule, with three chambers each holding two small black seeds.

The wood of box is yellow, hard, heavy, and even-grained. It is used for fine turnery, carving, engravings, and mathematical instruments. (The plant is not illustrated.)

Heath Family, Ericacesae.

122. Strawberry Tree,
Arbutus unedo

Called 'strawberry tree' from the obvious resemblance of its fruit to strawberries. Its ancient Irish names are *suglair* and *caithne*.

This rare tree grows wild around Killarney, Lough Gill, and a few other places in western Ireland. Rarely over twenty feet high, it forms thickets along the watersides. The leaves are alternate, simple, and oval, with toothed edges; they are evergreen, with a leathery texture, and are dark green above, pale green below.

The flowers, which open irregularly in autumn and winter, are white waxy bells, with five green sepals, five white petals united into a tube, ten stamens, and a five-celled ovary. They develop into juicy berries that take a whole year to ripen. The berries are at first white, then yellow, and finally red, and measure up to ½ in. across. The flesh is edible, but insipid. Birds take the berries and so spread the seeds.

The bark of the strawberry tree is reddish-brown and breaks away in flakes. The hard red-brown wood is used only for decorative carving. (The plant is not illustrated.)

Buttercup Family, Ranunculaceae.

123. Traveller's Joy,
Clematis vitalba

'Traveller's joy' is a literary or poetic name. This plant is also called 'old man's beard' from its hairy fruits, 'virgin's bower' from its habit of forming natural shelters of foliage, and 'wild clematis' from the Latin name.

The traveller's joy is found only on lime-rich soils, such as the chalk downs, but it is very common there. It has a stout woody stem with a rough fibrous bark, and scrambles over bushes and into treetops, often reaching a length of many yards. It bears compound leaves with 3–5 oval, pointed, leaflets, which have coarsely toothed or lobed edges. The pretty white flowers are about an inch across, and open in July or August. They are followed by hard seeds bearing masses of feathery hairs, and these persist on the naked stems after the leaves have been shed. (The plant is not illustrated.)

THE TREE'S WOOD

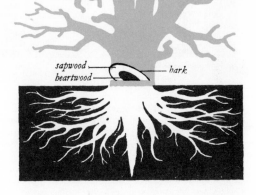

sapwood
heartwood
bark

Wood Structure

The stem of a tree in section consists on the outside of bark, which can be divided into three layers: *cork*, *green bark* and *bast*. Within lies the wood.

Between the inner part of the bark and the outer part of the wood there is a very narrow layer made up of living cells. This is the *cambium* or *growth layer* which, by the division of single cells, forms bark on its outer side and wood on its inner side. In all our common trees and bushes, this inward growth takes place in such a way that each year a new ring of wood is formed *outside* the old growth, and this method of formation causes the cambium to move outwards. The rings are called *annual rings*.

The single annual rings are not uniformly composed. In the spring when the tree is forming leaves and new shoots, the need for water is great, so that the portion of the annual ring produced during this period consists mainly of conductive tissues. In coniferous trees or softwoods, the conductive elements have thin walls and wide cavities. In broadleaved trees or hardwoods, there are also, besides the simple conductive elements, many large pores or vessels. All such wood is called *spring wood*.

Once the leaves and new shoots have been formed, there is less need for water-conducting tissue, and the wood now formed is more solid and consists mainly of thick-walled cells; in many broadleaved trees the vessels are fewer and smaller. This wood is called *summer wood*. On account of

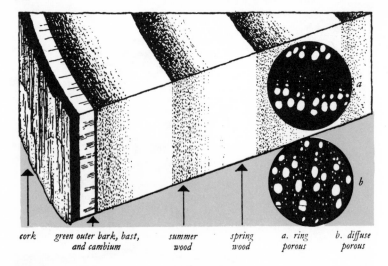

| cork | green outer bark, bast, and cambium | summer wood | spring wood | a. ring porous | b. diffuse porous |

these differences in structure, the boundaries of the different annual rings are clearly marked. Summer wood is usually darker than spring wood, and is stronger and harder, because of the denser structure.

Among the broadleaved trees, if the vessels (*pores*) which are first formed are considerably larger than those which are formed later, the wood is called *ring-porous* since rings of large pores can be seen. Examples of ring-porous woods are oak, ash and cherry. However, if the first-formed vessels are of approximately the same size as those which are produced later, and evenly spread through the wood, it is called *diffuse-porous*. Examples of diffuse-porous woods are beech, birch and walnut.

The width of the vessels (or pores) varies much from species to species, and hardwoods can be divided into those with *large pores*, e.g. oak, ash and walnut, and those with *fine pores* such as beech, birch and cherry.

The width of each annual ring depends on the growing conditions of the tree, and may vary considerably from under one-twentieth of an inch to over half-an-inch—even in the same tree, at different periods of its life.

In many trees changes in the inner wood occur with age, as the activities of life cease, and what is called the *heartwood*, consisting of dead cells, is formed. Usually the heartwood has a lower water content than the *sapwood* (see below) and its cells are blocked by '*tyloses*' (thin ingrowing structures) which are formed from storage cells outside them. Quite often dark-coloured substances are deposited in the heartwood, and this portion of the wood becomes clearly darker.

Heartwood is the more valuable part of the wood as it is more attractive and slightly stronger. The outer, paler, and functionally active wood is the *sapwood*. However, both heartwood and sapwood are used together, except for the more exacting work.

When the formation of heartwood has begun, it continues fairly regularly each year by the conversion of the innermost sapwood to heartwood, though this change does not always follow the course of the annual rings.

As a result of the different tensions which occur because a tree trunk, when drying, shrinks more around its outer circumference than it does towards its centre, wood used when unseasoned becomes warped like the boards illustrated. These boards are concave on the outer or sapwood side and convex on the inner or heartwood side. If boards of this kind, not fully seasoned, have to be glued together, for example to make a door, care must be taken that adjacent sapwood sides are turned so that each faces in the opposite direction, and the differences in dimensions thus tend to cancel each other out.

In a cross-section of the stem, fine stripes can be seen—often with the naked eye—running from the centre of the stem out to the bark. These stripes are called *rays*, and are made up of special cells; they serve both for the storage of nutrients and for the transport of these from the bark to the wood, and vice versa. Those rays which extend from the bark right into the centre are primary rays, while those which run only a certain way into the wood are secondary rays. The length and breadth of rays vary from species to species, and are important features in the identification of wood.

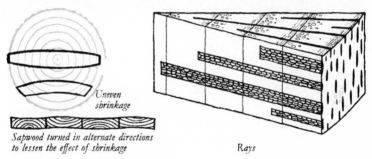

Uneven shrinkage

Sapwood turned in alternate directions to lessen the effect of shrinkage

Rays

Irregularities and faults in wood

Knots are the remains of the trees' branches. Most of them start at the very pith of the stem, and the growth layers of the branch are originally produced in conjunction with those of the stem. Indeed, the larger the branches are, the stouter the knots will be. Over the lower portion of the tree, the length and thickness of the knots increases the higher one goes up the stem, and the pattern formed by the distribution of knots thus resembles an inverted cone (see p. 204). But towards the tip of the tree, the knots, in common with the branches, get smaller again.

Knots of a particular type are called 'dead' knots, and come from branches that were dead *before* they were absorbed into the trunk.

Too many knots reduce the strength of the wood, and knot-free wood is especially in demand for exacting work; but it can only be cut from the outer layers of large trees.

Curly-grained wood is wood with twisted and wavy fibres, which is difficult to cleave and to work. It is highly valued for furniture veneers.

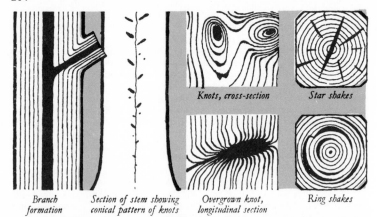

| Branch formation | Section of stem showing conical pattern of knots | Overgrown knot, longitudinal section | Ring shakes |

Knots, cross-section *Star shakes*

Spiral-grained wood is produced when the fibres are arranged spirally in relation to the axis of a tree. Such timber warps very easily.

Star shakes are cracks which begin in the pith and develop in a radial direction, apparently caused by varying tensions in the growing tree.

Ring shakes are cracks which follow one or more of the annual rings. These faults are often found in trees which have great variation in the width of their annual rings.

Bark in wood is due to creased (pleated) bark and fragments of bark which are ingrown and overgrown.

Frost cracks are longitudinal fissures in the stem. They arise when the outer wood, with greater moisture content, is affected by severe frost, and contracts more than the inner wood. Sometimes these cracks may be grown over by new annual rings, but they can nearly always be seen, as there is usually a thickening over the cracks.

The Elements of Wood

Wood consists of cells with various specialized functions.

(1) *Conducting tissue.* This consists of elongated cells. There are two types, *tracheids* (water tube cells) and *vessels* (water tubes); the latter are only found in the hardwoods, or timbers of broadleaved trees.

Tracheids are slender cells up to $\frac{1}{8}$ in. long, with woody walls. They are enclosed at the ends, but are connected with other cell types by pores in the side walls.

Vessels are larger structures specializing in water transport. They are formed of groups of cells which are connected lengthwise with each other, and the end walls of which are sometimes joined together. Thus vessels look like long woody tubes. In ash and oak for example, the tubes may be over a foot long. They are connected with each other, as with the tracheids and storage cells, by pores in the side walls.

(2) *Strengthening tissue.* This consists of wood fibres 1–2 mm. long, composed of longitudinal thick-walled cells which have a supporting or strengthening function, as have the vessels and tracheids to some degree.

(3) *Storage tissue*. Storage tissue consists of living cells called parenchyma cells, which are thin-walled, short and brick-shaped. They appear both in the rays and in the *wood parenchyma*. The function of the parenchyma cells is both to conduct nutrient substances through the wood and to store them.

The Tree's Nourishment

The cells of wood, like those of all green plants, are built up by the nutrition process called *photosynthesis*, i.e. the building up of substances with the help of light. Photosynthesis is the basis of all plant growth.

It takes place in the green leaves, which can be compared to factories, as the *carbon dioxide* in the air, in conjunction with the *water* rising up from the root, is converted to the organic substance *starch*. The energy for this formation of substance is provided by the sunlight. Moreover the surplus oxygen which is produced in this process is given off by the tree. Water drawn up from the roots provides the inorganic or mineral salts, nutrient substances which are necessary for the tree. These are carried up in the *rising* sap stream in the sapwood portion of the wood to the leaves, where they help to form organic substances that are then carried in the *downward* sugar sap stream of organic nutrients in the bast or inner layer of the bark. On the way a certain amount of material is used in the tree's height and girth growth, while the surplus is used by the roots.

Chlorophyll, the green-coloured matter which enables the leaves to utilize the energy provided by light, is contained both in cells inside the leaves and in labial cells which regulate the opening of the numerous *stomata* (pores) in the outer skin of the leaves. The air which provides the carbon dioxide is assimilated by means of these stomata.

To complete this account of the tree's growth, all its life processes in leaf, flower, stem, and root, derive their energy from the normal process of breathing, whereby oxygen from the air combines with carbon compounds (sugar, etc.), causing the release of carbon dioxide. This explains why there are breathing pores, called lenticels in the bark of all trees.

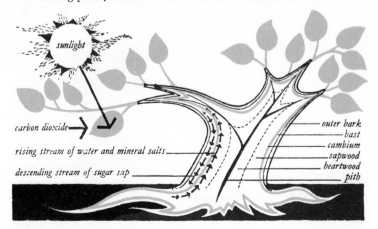

sunlight

carbon dioxide →

rising stream of water and mineral salts

descending stream of sugar sap

— *outer bark*
— *bast*
— *cambium*
— *sapwood*
— *heartwood*
— *pith*

DEVELOPMENT OF BRITISH FORESTS:

Year	Period	Main Plant Community	1	2	3	4	5	6
A.D. 2000	BEECH AGE	Planted Species						
	Sub-Atlantic **IX**	Beech forests / Oak forests / Pasture / Heath						
0 B.C. 400								
	OAK-ASH AGE	Oak forests / Fields						
	Sub-Boreal **VIII**	Grassland						
2500	OAK-ELM AGE							
	Atlantic **VII**	Mixed oak forests						
5500	PINE AGE							
	Boreal **VI** **V**	Pine forests						
	Pre-Boreal **IV**							
8000	TUNDRA AGE							
9000	*Later Dryas* **III**	Tundra scrub						
	Alleröd **II**	Light forests						
10000								
	Earlier Dryas **I**	Treeless tundra						
15000	ICE AGE	Ice covering						

PRE-HISTORY TO THE PRESENT DAY

| 7 | 8 | 9 | 10 | 11 | 12 13 14 15 16 | 17 18 | 19 20 |

1 . . . . . Herbs
2 Dwarf birch   Arctic willow   Dryas
3 . . . Crowberry
4 . . . . Heather
5 . . . . . Juniper
6 . . . . . . Aspen
7 . . . . . . Birch
8 . . . Scots pine
9 . . . . . . Hazel
10 Common alder

11 . . . . Oak
12 . . . . Elm
13 . . . . . . Lime
14 . . . . Ash
15 Norway maple
16 . . . . . . Beech
17 . . . Hornbeam
18 Norway spruce
19 . . . . Ivy
20 . . . . Mistletoe

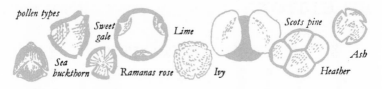

pollen types — *Sweet gale* — *Lime* — *Scots pine* — *Ash* — *Sea buckthorn* — *Ramanas rose* — *Ivy* — *Heather*

The forests of Britain have not always looked as they do today. The history of their development extends over a period of 17,000 years, and during this time changes in climate and methods of cultivation have had their effect.

Knowledge of this development is of great scientific interest and is based on the detailed findings of research work in a number of different fields. Geology, botany, zoology, archaeology, history, chemistry and physics have combined to give us the information which we have today.

The most important evidence of the forest and general plant growth of former times has been found in our bogs and lakes. Many of these are very old, and in the course of time trees, branches, leaves, flowers and fruits were deposited in such a way that the oldest deposits lie lowest and the youngest at the top, except where the digging of peat from the bogs or flowing water in the lakes has disturbed the layers.

By identifying these remains we can obtain a picture of the plants existing in the neighbourhood of bogs and lakes during the periods in question. However, these pictures may be very incomplete; many of the plant remains cannot be identified owing to the effect of time, and also, they only provide evidence of the species which grew in the immediate vicinity of the places investigated. Therefore we now use the *pollen analysis* method, which gives more definite results.

Pollen is the fertilizing dust produced by the stamens in the flowers of plants. In the case of most forest trees, pollen is dispersed by the wind and falls almost like rain on the countryside. The pollen grains of various plants can be distinguished from each other under the microscope, and moreover they are exceedingly resistant to the decomposition processes which occur throughout nature.

In tests from layers in bogs and lakes, the pollen grains from the different species have been counted, and from a comparison of results one may arrive with some certainty at an assessment of the composition of forests throughout the ages.

Just as the interior of Greenland is now covered with ice, so large ice masses covered northern Europe during the three Ice Ages. The last of these terminated about 15000 B.C.; then began the development of vegetation which we can trace down to the present time.

The diagram on pages 206–207 gives a picture of the development of forests from 15000 B.C. until the present day. It is a pollen diagram and shows graphically the percentage proportion between the pollen of the different tree species, and of the herb flora during the various periods.

The column on the extreme left gives the year, the next column states the names of the periods. After this the most important plant communities are shown, and finally there is the actual pollen diagram.

Period I. *Earlier Dryas Period* (15000–10000 B.C.) (named after *Dryas octopetala*, then widespread). Arctic climate. Large barren areas. Sedges, grasses, mosses, lichens, dryas, scattered juniper, dwarf and hairy birch (some sea buckthorn).

Period II. *Alleröd Period* (10000–9000 B.C.) (named after the place where the type of mud which characterizes the geological period was first observed). Sub-arctic (cool) climate. Light forests of hairy birch, aspen and juniper (some Scots pine). First footprints of man.

Period III. *Later Dryas Period* (9000–8000 B.C.). Arctic climate again. Tundra again, with dwarf birch, arctic willow, dryas, and scattered hairy birch scrub. The *Late Glacial Age* ends with this period and is followed by the *Post-Glacial Age*.

Dryas, *Dryas octopetala*

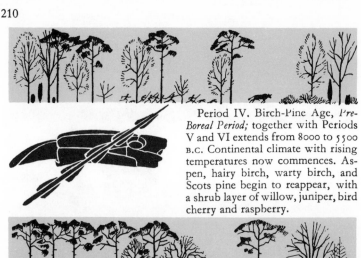

Period IV. Birch-Pine Age, *Pre-Boreal Period;* together with Periods V and VI extends from 8000 to 5500 B.C. Continental climate with rising temperatures now commences. Aspen, hairy birch, warty birch, and Scots pine begin to reappear, with a shrub layer of willow, juniper, bird cherry and raspberry.

Period V. Pine-Hazel Age, *Boreal Period.* Warm continental climate. Extensive pine and hazel forests. Appearance of elm, oak, small-leaved lime and common alder, guelder rose, mistletoe and ivy.

Period VI. Transition period to Oak-Elm Age, *Boreal Period.* Warm continental climate. Steadily extending pine and hazel forests with curve for common alder rising sharply. Similarly elm and oak come to the fore. Appearance of alder buckthorn and dogwood. Percentage of herb pollen falls sharply as the herb community is displaced by the forest community. Continental period ends and climate changes at the end of the period to a coastal climate with greater rainfall and milder winters.

Period VII. Oak and Elm Forest Age, *Atlantic Period* (5500–2500 B.C.). Warm coastal climate. Scots pine falls back; oak, elm and lime gain further ground. Underwood of hazel, common alder, wild cherry, hawthorn, guelder rose, raspberry and holly. Mistletoe and ivy are common.

Period VIII. Oak and Ash Forest Age, *Sub-Boreal Period* (2500–400 B.C.). Climate more continental with colder winters, but settled warm summers. Ivy loses ground, but mistletoe remains constant. Elm and lime recede, and oak dominates the forest picture; interspersed ash is present. Hazel is very prominent. Men clear the forest and cultivate the ground, heather spreads, and pollen of various types of corn and plantain occurs.

At the end of this period the summer temperatures fall and the climate becomes very dry; post-glacial warm period ends.

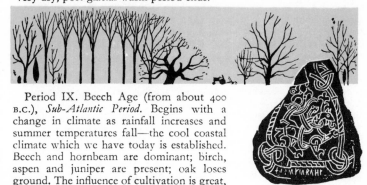

Period IX. Beech Age (from about 400 B.C.), *Sub-Atlantic Period*. Begins with a change in climate as rainfall increases and summer temperatures fall—the cool coastal climate which we have today is established. Beech and hornbeam are dominant; birch, aspen and juniper are present; oak loses ground. The influence of cultivation is great, as shown by the high pollen percentage of heather and cultivated plants.

Man and Forests

In addition to the effect of variations in climate, the human race, with its changing utilization of land, has had a considerable influence on the development of forests throughout Britain.

The first people who penetrated the northern countries were both hunters and fishers whose activities left no mark on the forests. But with the dawn of the later or Neolithic Stone Age a people who cultivated the land first came on the scene, and the clearing of forest land began. The forests were cleared in order to make fields, and to provide food for cattle. Clearings were made partly by burning forests, but mainly by felling with flint axes, which at this time became important as cutting tools. In many places the final phase of this forest clearing was a very open and devastated hardwood forest of oak, birch, alder and hazel, with a ground vegetation of grass. When the land in such a clearing was no longer fruitful it was abandoned, and it then reverted to forest.

A second forest clearing period began in the Iron Age. Iron axes were so effectively and extensively used in the last part of the Iron Age, the time of the Anglo-Saxon and Viking migrations, that the forests were laid waste on a large scale. The curve for herb pollen rises sharply in the pollen diagram. The forests were thinned and became wind-blown and the soil condition deteriorated so that regrowth was impeded. In some regions the forests were replaced by heathlands, but grass-covered pastures became common elsewhere. Both heathlands and pastures would again have been liable to revert to forest, but this was prevented by the grazing of cattle and by cultivation; also, on the heaths, by fires deliberately lit, often annually, to get a transitory improvement of the spring grazing.

Our typical British landscape with open country, fields, heaths and scattered forest was formed at this time, though the hedgerows and hedgerow trees came later.

When the Normans arrived in 1066, most of England had already been divided into parishes, each with its grazed and cultivated fields. Most villages had also an expanse of waste land or forest where the people could cut firewood, graze their cattle, and put out their pigs in the acorn season Domesday Book records the existence of numerous village woodlands. Already the surviving forests were threatened, and the Normans strengthened the forest laws to protect both the deer and the trees.

As time went on, the protection of the many Royal Forests established by the Normans became less effective. For political or economic reasons most of these forests gradually passed from the ownership of the Crown into the hands of the great land-owning families, and almost invariably their devastation followed.

There were many reasons for this devastation. Until about 1550 houses in the country were built entirely of timber, and large quantities were required for building castles and forts as well as mills, bridges and harbours; most of the wood used was heavy oak timber.

Shipbuilding increased from about 1500, and large amounts of timber, especially oak, were required for building ships for the navy. About 2,000 large oak trees were needed to build a single ship of the line. In addition, large quantities of wood were used for fuel. Wood was also used as charcoal in the iron industry and in the manufacture of glass, gunpowder, bricks and tiles.

Although so much wood was used in these ways, it was the keeping of stock and the cutting down of brushwood for fences which were mainly responsible for the deterioration of the forests.

Cattle were liable to overrun the countryside and therefore cultivated fields had to be enclosed so that the crops were not damaged. The commonest method of enclosure was a fence of staves or stakes composed of two rows of stakes, up to 6 ft. apart, with the intervening space filled up with branches and twigs.

These fences seldom lasted more than one year, since in the winter, when the supply of ordinary fuel ran short, the brushwood from the fences was used for burning. In the spring new material was cut for the fences and every year the process was repeated. In this way, very large areas of scrub and young trees were destroyed.

The grazing of livestock in the forests was equally harmful. Cows, sheep, goats and horses had to find food in the forest, with the result that all young plants, as well as buds and the young shoots of older trees as high as the animals could reach, were eaten. In places like Richmond Park one can see today what the grazed forest must have looked like, without undergrowth and with the typical bitten-off crowns.

Only pigs contributed to the regrowth—especially of beech—by their churning of the soil when looking for beech mast or acorns.

These processes of forest destruction led inevitably to local shortages of brushwood, firewood, and timber, and by the fifteenth century many landowners were taking steps to safeguard what remained of their woods. They did this by a method called *coppicing*, from the French *couper*, to cut. Whenever a block of woodland was cut over, they enclosed it with fences for at least seven years, so that the young shoots, secure from grazing livestock and wanton cutting, could make good growth undisturbed.

Only broadleaved trees will send up fresh shoots from their stumps, but over most of England the coppice system produced, for hundreds of years, ample supplies of poles and rods for fences and hurdles, and also firewood and charcoal wood, at a profit to the landowners. The main trees so grown were hazel, hornbeam, ash, birch, beech, alder, and sweet chestnut. Because the shoots from the stumps seldom grew big enough to yield building timber, the custom arose of leaving selected seedling trees, usually of oak or ash, to grow up with the coppice, and these were not cut until they were well-grown, and perhaps a hundred years old. They were called *standard* trees, and the system is known as *coppice-with-standards*.

In Scotland, Wales, the Lake District, Devon and Cornwall, and also in Ireland, oak was the main coppice tree. It could only be coppiced every twenty years or so, but it gave a good yield of stout poles, charcoal wood, and valuable bark for tanning leather. Nearly all the oakwoods of our western hills, often mistakenly regarded as 'natural' by botanists or dismissed as 'scrub' by foresters, are in fact abandoned coppices which were managed on an orderly and profitable plan for several hundred years.

Gradually, as more and more land became permanently enclosed for farming, the dead hedges of brushwood were replaced by walls, banks, or the live hedges of hawthorn that are such a feature of our countryside.

This development reduced the need for brushwood and hurdles, while the growing use of coal and eventually of oil lessened the demand for firewood and charcoal wood. Oak tanbark was largely replaced by imported bark and wood extracts. Few coppices are now profitable; most are being converted to plantations, leaving *copse* on the map to puzzle the historians.

Modern forestry is based on the plantation system, whereby young trees are raised from seed in nurseries and planted out fairly closely, about five feet apart, so that some 1,750 stand on each acre of ground. As they grow bigger, some are thinned out to yield small poles, while the better ones are kept to become full-sized timber trees. Often these are 100 years old, and 100 feet tall, before they are felled, and only one hundred or so survive to the end, on each acre. Both coniferous trees, or softwoods (illustrated on pages 17 to 37) and broadleaved trees, or hardwoods, can be grown as timber crops in this way.

The raising of forest trees from seed is a very old craft that began with the monasteries. The first skilled forester of whom we have a record was William the Cellarer, surnamed Blair, who as long ago as 1460 was raising ash, birch, willow, broom and hawthorn in nursery beds at Coupar Angus Abbey in Perthshire.

The dissolution of the monasteries in Tudor times, and the enclosure movement that led to the hedged fields mentioned earlier, put much wealth and power into the hands of the landowners. Their usual practice was to afforest some of their poorer ground, under the care of estate foresters, with several objects in view. Well planned woods gave them a convenient timber supply, a source of income from the sales of wood, shelter for farms, cover for game, and a fine landscape setting for their great houses. From the sixteenth century right down to the present day, private landowners have been actively tending and extending parks, shelterbelts and plantations, using oak, ash, beech, sycamore, Scots pine, larch, Norway spruce, and some of the more recently introduced conifers.

In consequence, our woodlands are both well dispersed and varied in character, and hold a good range of timbers. It is usual for many fine specimen trees, often of rare kinds introduced from overseas, to be grouped around great houses. The whole pattern, though so pleasing to the eye, is essentially artificial, like the hedgerows that extend the feeling of the wooded landscape among the fields. The privately owned woods embrace two and a half million acres, or about one-twentieth of our land surface, and combine a wealth of beauty with a valuable reserve of timber; the private owners are currently planting 30,000 acres each year.

Early in the present century people began to realize that there were good prospects for extending the forests on a larger scale, as a national enterprise. The clearance of the natural forests had freed much good land for agriculture, but it had also left bare and waste great expanses of moorland and hillside that were of no use for cultivation, nor even for profitable grazing. Meanwhile an enormous demand had arisen, in the growing cities, for wood of all kinds, and for wood products such as paper, and this was being met largely by imports. Therefore, in 1919, the Forestry Commission was set up, to plant and develop woodlands for timber production in line with modern needs. By 1960, the Forestry Commission had formed five hundred new forests in all parts of Great Britain, and had planted one and a quarter million acres of young trees, equivalent to one-fortieth of the total land area. Its current programme calls for planting a further 60,000 acres each year, involving over one hundred million young trees.

Similar developments, on a parallel scale, are taking place in Northern Ireland, the Irish Republic, and the Isle of Man.

These new forests are being formed on land of low quality, and there it is found that coniferous trees, or softwoods, thrive much better, and yield timber far faster, than do the broadleaved ones or hardwoods. Moreover, while the demand for hardwood timber has remained constant, and can largely be met from privately-owned woods, there is a great and growing market for softwoods in many forms—building timber, box-making, railway sleepers, telegraph poles, pit props, chipboard, hardboard, insulation board, wood wool, and above all for paper pulp.

To get the trees that will grow best in our oceanic climate, the foresters have gone to the Pacific coast of North America for Douglas fir, Sitka spruce, giant and noble firs, lodgepole pine, Lawson cypress, western hemlock, and western red cedar. They have also brought Japanese larch, Corsican pine, European larch and Norway spruce from their homelands, and expanded the planting of our native Scots pine. Over four-fifths of the planting, on private estates as well as in the Commission's forests, is now being done with these thirteen coniferous trees. However, a good deal of oak, ash, beech and sycamore are still being planted on the better soils; elm, poplar, and willow find a place amid really fertile farmlands, and many other ornamental broadleaved trees are grown in parks and gardens.

FOREST TREE BREEDING

Genetics, or the science of breeding, has been applied to forestry, just as to gardening and agriculture, but forest tree breeding began at a far more recent date.

The basis of all breeding of improved strains is variation, both great and small. Beech trees in a forest show many differences if closely observed. It is evident that the date of leafing varies from tree to tree, so that some trees come into leaf late and others early, and a similar variation occurs as regards leaf fall. Moreover the form of trees varies. Some trees clearly have a main axis, i.e. a straight stem continuing to the top, while in other trees the stem is quickly lost in the branches of the crown. In many trees the angle between the branches and the stem is acute, which causes long knots. In others the branch angle is less acute, and the knots are shorter.

These variations are hereditary, and this can be proved by collecting seed from an early-leafing beech, sowing the seed, and observing whether there are any early-leafing beech among the progeny. It will now be obvious that some, though not all, of the trees have been pollinated by other early-leafing beeches. In order to be more certain of an early-leafing progeny, one must therefore artificially cross two different early-leafing beeches.

The founder of the hereditary school was the Austrian Augustinian monk, Gregor Mendel. In the years 1857–64, by systematic crossing

216

experiments, especially with peas, he established the laws which govern the segregation of characteristics in related descendants. It is evident from these Mendelian principles of segregation that differing potentialities are inherited in a definite manner, which applies to both plants and animals.

It is the potentiality which is inherited, not the characteristics; the latter may or may not come to light, depending on exterior conditions, that is, on the environment.

This means that there is a difference between the potential character (genotype) and the apparent character (phenotype). The apparent character is always to be seen, while the potential character, derived from the accumulation of inherited genes, will be evident only if conditions allow it to be so. This principle was expressed in another way by the famous Danish geneticist, W. Johansen: 'the phenotype is the normal reaction of the genotype according to the given exterior conditions'.

The following example illustrates this problem. A red-flowered race of a particular *Primula* species is discovered. If a plant of this type is moved to a greenhouse with a high temperature, the flowers produced afterwards are white. External conditions, involving in this case a high temperature, have altered the appearance of the plant, i.e. the apparent character.

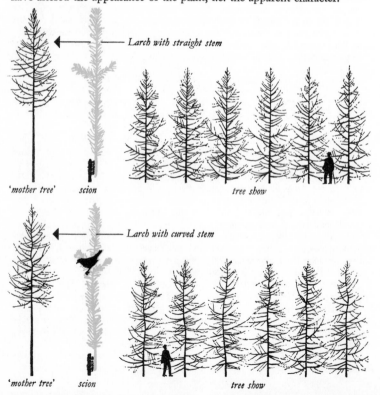

'mother tree'   scion   ← *Larch with straight stem*   *tree show*

'mother tree'   scion   ← *Larch with curved stem*   *tree show*

However, the potential character remains unchanged, as is shown by the fact that such a plant will again produce red flowers when it is moved to a place with a lower temperature. Moreover the progeny obtained from the seed of a plant with flowers which changed to white, or from that of a normal red-flowered variety, will both produce red flowers in a normal temperature and white in higher temperatures. Thus only the apparent character is changed; the potential character is unchanged.

The type of beech which is valuable to foresters, a tree with a long straight stem, is very much a product of hereditary and environment. When we consider the tree we can only judge from its apparent character. If we are to find out what it contains we must investigate it more closely. This can be done in several ways. One method is to collect seed from the tree, sow this seed, and judge the tree from the progeny obtained. But this is a long and difficult process, for trees grow slowly, as we know, and it is difficult to assess them solely from the growth produced in youth.

Another method is to test trees in what is called a 'tree show'. This is done by taking scions from the trees to be compared and grafting them on root stocks under the same conditions, so that grafts of one tree form one line and those of another tree form a different line. In this way the differences will be clearly shown, and one will be in a position to select the tree which has the required characteristics. (See illustrations, page 216.)

A collection of plants formed by the vegetative propagation (grafting, cuttings, layering or division) of a single individual is called a *clone*, and examples from horticulture may be given of clones or varieties of apples, strawberries and potatoes.

Clones of forest trees are seldom used directly in the forest, but are now to be found in the Forestry Commission's seed orchards. Clones of two or more good trees are allowed to pollinate each other, and seed is thus collected which has every possibility of yielding good plants.

GREAT TREES

Although in Britain there are no trees which, by American standards, could be called giant specimens, there are nevertheless some trees of considerable size in our forests and parks. It is difficult for trees to attain giant dimensions in the British forests because of the constant wind which exerts unceasing pressure on the crowns and is greater in proportion as a tree grows above the height of the surrounding stand, and also because it is only with age that trees reach really large sizes. From the point of view of forest economics it does not pay to allow trees to stand after they have reached a certain age; this age varies for different species, but is determined to some degree by the point at which rate of growth begins to fall off.

The giant trees which are nevertheless to be found in our forests, owe their existence in every case to the fact that they have been preserved on aesthetic grounds by owners who respect the natural beauty of the countryside and—in many cases—by the people concerned with the forest without any thought of utilization or profit.

Two of our tallest trees are Douglas firs. One at Powis Castle near Welshpool is 181 ft. high, and is the highest specimen in Wales and all Britain. The other, at Duncraig in Wester Ross, measures 180 ft. and is one of the highest trees in Scotland. The tallest tree in England is a wellingtonia (*Sequoiadendron giganteum*), introduced from California and growing at Endsleigh, near Tavistock in Devon; this is 162 ft. tall.

Also in this record-breaking class is the famous silver fir at Kilbride, near Inveraray in Argyll, which is 180 ft. tall and 20½ ft. round at breast height. A stem with these dimensions holds, in the forester's customary measure, around 2,250 cubic feet hoppus, one of the biggest timber volumes ever recorded in the British Isles. The weight of this stem as it stands in the living, unseasoned condition, is around 75 tons. (Hoppus, or quarter-girth, measure, is the conventional system of measuring round logs and standing trees developed by Edward Hoppus, a surveyor who published ready-reckoners in about 1730. One hoppus foot equals 1·273 true cubic feet.)

Our heaviest stand of timber is the Leighton Redwood Grove, which is close to Welshpool and belongs to the Royal Forestry Society of England and Wales. These redwoods are of the coastal species, *Sequoia sempervirens*, and were brought over from California nearly one hundred years ago. They are now over 112 ft. tall, with an average girth of 11 ft., and the stand holds over 24,000 hoppus feet to the acre. This may be compared with the 4,000 hoppus feet found in a normal mature pinewood, though it must be added that the figure for the redwoods includes their very thick bark.

The tallest tree in Ireland is a Sitka spruce at Curraghmore, County Waterford, measuring 166 ft. tall by 18 ft. round. Ireland's stoutest tree is another Sitka spruce at Caledon Castle, Armagh, which though only 144 ft. high is 23 ft. round.

All these record-breaking trees are conifers, and all have been introduced from abroad and planted within the last hundred years. How do our native trees, and particularly the broadleaved ones, compare?

Our tallest broadleaved tree is a common lime, 152 ft. high, at Duncombe Park in Yorkshire. But when it comes to girth and sheer bulk the ancient oaks lead the way. There is a pollard oak at Manton in Cheshire which is 43 ft. round, and even stouter ones are recorded in the past, such as Damory's Oak in Dorset, which was 68 ft. round. The Golynos Oak felled at Bassaleg Farm near Monmouth in 1810, yielded 2,426 hoppus feet of timber; it was then found to be 400 years old.

No other broadleaved trees equal the oaks for girth or longevity, but a native conifer, the yew, can grow almost as stout and last even longer. Our biggest living yew, at Ulcombe churchyard in Kent, is 34½ ft. in girth; but one that stood in Fortingall churchyard, Perthshire, in 1771, was no less than 56 ft. round. From what we know of the slow outward growth of yew trunks, we can safely say that these are over 2,000 years old.

To complete our records, Ireland's largest broadleaved tree is a horse chestnut at Inishtioge, County Kilkenny, 105 ft. tall by 21 ft. in girth. The stoutest surviving tree in Wales is the Park Plain Oak at Powis Castle, 40 ft. round. The stoutest tree recorded in Scotland in recent times is a Scots pine at Guisachan, near Glen Affric, Inverness-shire, which scaled 24 ft. round.

LATIN-ENGLISH GLOSSARY

acutifolius: sharp-leaved.
alba: white.
alpinus: belonging to mountains.
aquifolium: with pointed leaves.
atrovirens: dark green.
aucuparia: used by fowlers.
aurita: eared.
avium: of the birds.
baccata: berried.
borealis: northern.
caesius: blue-green.
campestre: belonging to the fields.
canadensis: Canadian.
candicans: shining white.
canescens: becoming grey.
carpinifolius: with leaf like hornbeam.
cathartica: purging.
cerasifera: bearing cherries.
cinerea: ashen grey.
coetanea: even-aged.
coerulea: heavenly blue.
communis: common.
concolor: single colour (leaf surfaces).
contorta: crooked.
cordata: heart-shaped.
daphnoides: laurel-like.
decidua: falling away.
effusa: spreading.
europaeus: European.
excelsior: taller.
fragilis: brittle.
fruticosus: bushy.
germanica: German.
glaucus: blue-grey.
glutinosa: sticky.
grandis: great.
helix: crooked.
hippocastanum: horse-chestnut.
hybrida: hybrid.
incana: pale grey.
insititia: grafted.
integerrima: entire-edged.
intermedia: intermediate.
laevis: smooth.
leptolepis: fine-scaled.
melanocarpa: black-fruited.
monogyna: having a single carpel.
montana: of the mountains.

nana: dwarf.
nigra: black.
occidentalis: from the west (America as contrasted with Asia).
opulus: tree name, probably maple.
oxyacanthoides: sharp-thorned.
padus: Greek name for a shrub.
palustris: belonging to swamps.
pentandra: five-stamened.
periclymenum: Greek name for climbing plant.
petraea: belonging to the rocks.
pimpinellifolius: with leaf like pimpernel.
platanoides: resembling a plane tree.
platyphyllos: broad-leaved.
plicatus: folded together.
pseudoplatanus: false plane.
pubescens: downy.
pumila: dwarf.
pungens: sharp.
racemosa: having flowers in spikes.
repens: creeping.
rhamnoides: like a buckthorn bush.
rivularis: belonging to stream-sides.
robur: sturdy.
rubra: red.
rugosa: wrinkled.
salicifolia: willow-leaved.
sanguinea: blood-red.
scoparius: broom-like.
serotina: late, backward.
sorbifolia: rowan-leaved.
sitchensis: from Sitka (Alaska).
spicata: like an ear of corn.
spinosa: having spines.
strobus: whorled (relates to cones).
taxifolia: yew-leaved.
tremula: shaking.
trichocarpa: hairy-fruited.
torminalis: good for colic.
uva-crispa: gooseberry.
verrucosa: warty.
viminalis: osier-like.
viridis: green.
vulgaris: common.
xylosteum: having bone-hard wood.

GLOSSARY OF BOTANICAL TERMS

See also diagrams on pp. 5–16, illustrating these and other technical terms.

Acuminate: tapering suddenly to a point.

Adventitious: arising through some favourable chance, away from the main system.

Alternate: set singly (not in pairs).

Anthers: male, pollen-bearing organs of a flower; actual heads of stamens.

Apomict: plant reproduced by seed, but without fertilization.

Apophysis: upper, exposed surface.

Auricle: ear-shaped projection of a leaf.

Axil: angle between two shoots, or between a shoot and a leaf.

Bark: hard protective outer layer of stem.

Bast: (1) conductive tissue between true wood and outer bark of a tree, which carries sugar sap down to the roots.
(2) fibres obtained from inner bark of certain trees, e.g. lime.

Bay: hollow between lobes of a leaf.

Berry: succulent fruit holding many seeds.

Bract: leaf-like structure, at base of leaf or cone-scale.

Bristle: hair developed into a sharp, protective body.

Calyx: outer whorl of a flower, composed of sepals.

Cambium: growth layer between bast and wood (wood cambium), or just below bark (cork cambium).

Canker: open wound on tree caused by fungus or bacterium.

Capsule: hard dry pod holding many seeds.

Carpel: seed-producing portion of flower; part or whole of an ovary.

Catkin: cluster of small wind-pollinated flowers.

Clone: group of plants raised vegetatively from one parent.

Compound: composed of many leaflets or carpels.

Cone: woody fruiting body of a coniferous or softwood tree.

Coppice: crop of poles raised by cutting back broadleaved trees to ground level to get many new shoots.

Cordate: shaped like a conventional heart.

Corolla: whorl of petals.

Cotyledon: seed leaf.

Cutting: portion of a plant cut from another one, for rooting.

Cyme: flower cluster with oldest flower in centre.

Dioecious: having flowers of separate sexes on separate plants.

Drupe: fruit wherein a single hard stone is surrounded by soft flesh and a firm skin.

Entire: simple, not divided.

Epicormic: arising from outer layers of wood.

Fascicle: bundle (of needles, etc.).

Flushing: breaking into leaf.

Fruit: seed-holding structure produced by a single flower; may hold one or many seeds.

Glabrous: smooth, hairless.

Gland: fleshy structure on a stem or leaf.

Glaucous: bluish green.

Graft: portion of one plant made to grow on another plant.

Hard seed: seed that does not germinate readily unless rubbed, boiled or chipped.

Heartwood: wood at the heart of the tree, transformed by chemical changes due to ageing; no longer carries sap.

Hermaphrodite: holding organs of

both sexes, i.e. stamens and ovary.

Hybrid: tree arising through cross-breeding between tree species.

Inflorescence: flower cluster.

Knot: remains of a branch, buried within wood.

Laciniate: deeply cut into many sections.

Lanceolate: lance-shaped, long and narrow.

Lateral: side.

Lenticel: breathing pore, on tree bark, etc.

Liana: woody plant with a pliant, non-rigid stem, which trails and needs support.

Linear: long and very narrow.

Lobed: partially divided into several sections.

Long shoot: normal shoot that increases length of branch.

Mast: heavy seed crop; seed.

Monoecious: having flowers of separate sexes, but on the same plant.

Monopodial: growing longer directly, from terminal bud.

Mycelium: thread or stem of fungus.

Nectar: gland secreting nectar.

Needle: narrow leaf.

Nodule: swelling on tree root, containing fungus or bacterium.

Nurse tree: tree planted to shelter another, more valuable, kind.

Nut: hard, dry, seed; borne singly.

Obovate: egg-shaped, but blunt towards tip.

Opposite: set in facing pairs.

Oval: egg-shaped, blunt towards base.

Ovary: seed bearing (female) portion of flower, composed of one or more carpels.

Ovule: single seed-element in or on a carpel.

Palmate: spreading outwards from a centre, like the fingers of the hand.

Panicle: open flower cluster, having the youngest flower at the tip.

Perianth: sepals and petals considered together.

Peduncle: flower (or fruit) stalk.

Pericarp: main covering layer of a succulent fruit, especially of a drupe; e.g. the flesh around a plum stone.

Petal: conspicuous leaf of a corolla.

Pinnate: divided in a feather-like fashion, i.e. with several leaflets or lobes set on either side of a central stalk.

Pinnatifid: split into pinnate sections.

Pistil: complete female organ of a flower, comprising the basal ovary, the style or stalk, and the stigma or tip.

Pith: soft tissue at very centre of a woody stem.

Pollard: tree cut back at about head height.

Pollination: fertilization of an ovule by pollen from a stamen.

Pome: fleshy fruit with several seeds grouped centrally — as in an apple.

Prickle: sharp structure developed from a surface hair.

Prostrate: creeping over the ground.

Raceme: long flower cluster with youngest flowers at tip.

Ray: band of wood tissue set radially in stem.

Receptacle: swollen end of flower stalk, bearing carpels, etc.

Recurved: bent back, particularly at the tip or edge.

Reflexed: bent back.

Revolute: turned over.

Rust: fungal disease on leaf, showing as discoloured patches.

Sapwood: outer, unaltered wood, still carrying sap upwards.

Scale: leaf-like structure.

Seed: ripe, reproductive element, developed from a single ovule.

Sepal: outer, leaf-like member of a flower.

Serrate: toothed, having an edge like a saw-blade.

Sessile: stalkless, and hence sitting directly on a branch.

Short shoot: modified shoot, bearing leaves or flowers, which does not increase the branch length.

Spine: sharp structure formed by a modified shoot or stipule.

Springwood: soft, pale, band of wood, with many conducting elements, laid down in spring.

Stamen: male organ of a flower, bearing pollen.

Stigma: receptive tip of a style, which catches pollen.

Stipule: small leaf-like organ at base of leaf.

Stomata: minute breathing pores on the surface of a leaf.

Stool shoot: coppice shoot arising from a stump.

Style: projecting organ of a carpel.

Summerwood: hard, dark, band of wood, with much structural tissue, laid down in summer.

Sympodial: growing longer indirectly, from a side bud.

Thorn: sharp organ formed from a modified shoot.

Translucent: allowing light to show through.

Truncate: cut off sharply.

Umbel: broad flat flower cluster, with youngest flower in centre.

Umbo: projection on cone scale.

Unisexual: having organs of only one sex, i.e. carpels or stamens.

Vessel: conductive element, composed of many cells, in the wood of a broadleaved tree, or hardwood.

Viscid: sticky.

Wart: woody swelling on a twig.

INDEX

This index shows the **key number** *of each tree, under both English and Latin names. The more important synonyms are in brackets.*